Get Wise to Your Advisor

*How to Reach Your
Investment Goals Without
Getting Ripped Off*

Steven D. Lockshin

WILEY

Cover image: iStockphoto / David Franklin
Cover design: Paul McCarthy

Published by John Wiley & Sons, Inc., Hoboken, New Jersey.
Published simultaneously in Canada.

For general information on our other products and services or for technical support, please
contact our Customer Care Department within the United States at (800) 762-2974,
outside the United States at (317) 572-3993 or fax (317) 572-4002.

Wiley publishes in a variety of print and electronic formats and by print-on-demand.
Some material included with standard print versions of this book may not be included in
e-books or in print-on-demand. If this book refers to media such as a CD or DVD that
is not included in the version you purchased, you may download this material at
http://booksupport.wiley.com. For more information about Wiley products,
visit www.wiley.com.

Library of Congress Cataloging-in-Publication Data:

Lockshin, Steven D.
    Get wise to your advisor : how to reach your investment goals without getting ripped
off / Steven D. Lockshin.
        pages   cm
    Includes index.
    ISBN 978-1-118-70073-0 (cloth); ISBN 978-1-118-70069-3 (ebk);
    ISBN 978-1-118-69886-0 (ebk)
        1. Investment advisors.   2. Financial services industry—Evaluation.
3. Investments.   4. Portfolio management.   5. Finance, Personal.   I. Title.
HG4621.L54 2013
332.6—dc23
                                                                              2013013314

Printed in the United States of America
10 9 8 7 6 5 4 3 2 1

To my wife, Allison, my "true north"
and the ultimate fiduciary in my life.

Contents

Preface

As I write these words, a battle is playing out in Washington, DC. This David-versus-Goliath contest pits investors against the investment brokerage industry—and it's not looking good for investors.

In the wake of the 2008 market crash and the ensuing financial crisis, lawmakers directed the Securities and Exchange Commission—Wall Street's cop—to hold stock and insurance brokers to a tough investor protection standard. The brokerage and insurance industries went ballistic, launching an all-out effort to delay, water down, and otherwise smother the coming standard before it could breathe a breath of mature life.

How exactly would this frightful new standard impact Wall Street? It would force brokers to put clients' interests first and it would likely make them liable if they profited unjustly at the cost of the average investor. That might seem like a good, commonsense idea to you and me. But Wall Street thinks very, very differently.

I want to be clear that many Wall Street brokers are truly concerned with doing the right thing for their clients. But as you'll learn, even the good guys operate in an industry so riddled with conflicts of interest that the temptation to put profits before people exerts a powerful and constant pull. This tainted environment is enabled by the regulatory standard that the industry is fighting tooth and nail to protect, a mushy standard that allows brokers a ton of, to put it politely, ethical wiggle room. Replacing that standard, the industry fears, will hurt its profit margins. And on Wall Street, profit margins are not, repeat *not*, to be messed with. After all, Wall Street, too, has its own investors to serve.

The bad news for consumers is that right now, the brokerage industry appears to have the upper hand in its struggle with an SEC weakened by turnover and trapped in inertia.

For now, Wall Street—which is the first place consumers look when they need investment and financial advice—has those consumers right where it wants them. Make no mistake, much of the guidance that is so lucrative for brokers is demonstrably damaging to investors. Often, the investment product that's not quite right for the client is *oh-so-right* for the broker because of the fat sales compensation that's at stake.

And even when investors catch on to the fact that they've been wronged, they too often find little recourse. The typical investor unwittingly signs away his right to sue when he signs a brokerage contract. Instead, such investors are granted the ability to pursue arbitration through a potentially lengthy and expensive process that is controlled by FINRA, the brokerage industry's self-regulator. Understandably, many investors don't even bother.

I am writing this book because things don't have to be this way. You, the consumer, have the power to stop it. And once you learn exactly how Wall Street operates—how your best interests are so often placed secondary to profits—I'm confident that you will send a message to the establishment by refusing to go along with the status quo. You, as an individual consumer, can help to tilt that status quo toward a new reality—a reality in which the needs of the consumer are placed first.

My goal, as the title says, is to wise you up. Part of my job in doing that is to pull back the veil on Wall Street (as well as non-Wall Street offenders who serve their needs before yours). After you read this book, you'll understand just how conflicted the mainstream brokerage industry is. You'll learn how the brokers, regulators, and lobbyists cooperate to enrich themselves and the industry at the consumers' expense. And you'll discover Wall Street's chameleon personality—how brokers and the big firms they work for confuse and mislead consumers into believing they're your allies.

But this isn't just another salacious look at how Wall Street's sausage is made. Most of that information is out there in one form or another. My mission in writing this book is also to provide information that can empower you. Simply stated, there *are* trustworthy financial advisors out there. It is possible to weed out conflicted advisors and find the ones that have the qualifications, the ethical standards, and the objectivity to serve as truly valuable allies.

At this point you may be asking yourself, "What does *he* have to gain from writing this book? What's *his* angle?" I hope your skepticism is at least a little aroused—because consumers of investment and financial advice desperately need to be more skeptical. The answer is that, yes, I conceivably have something to gain in having you read this book. Inevitably, somebody may contact me because something in this small guide struck a cord with him or her.

In 1994 I founded what is now known as Convergent Wealth Advisors, an independent financial advisory firm based in Washington, DC and Los Angeles, and I have gone on to establish other financial service enterprises to serve investors of varied wealth. I started in this business more than two decades ago, driven to deliver institutional quality advice to individuals. It's been my mission to be the opposite of the conflicted "advisors" that this book will expose. My goal is to always be the type of advisor that I will hold up for praise in this book. Independent of product sales, true advisors act as fiduciaries, and we're fee-based rather than commission-based. As you read, you'll learn what all that means and why it's important. And, since I currently serve investors of varied size, there lies an inherent conflict in this book.

But here's a bit of context. I've worked in the industry for 20 years and have already enjoyed all I could ask for in terms of success. I built a firm that advises on over $11 billion of assets for the kind of clients most advisors would frankly give their left arm for. *Barron's* has ranked me the top independent advisor in the nation. I've benefited from all of the exposure and success that I could want. Trust me, I'm not hustling for your business, and if I were, there are definitely easier ways of doing that than writing a book.

The truth is that my goal is larger than my personal interests or those of my business. You see, the relationship between consumers and the brokerage industry truly bothers me. I see it as a form of social injustice. The cynical and damaging way that the industry treats individuals and families is just wrong, and after observing the industry up close for two decades, I know too much to keep quiet. That's especially true because I know that consumers, like you, do have the ability to reclaim control of their financial futures.

At its core, this book is intended to empower you, the consumer. When you've finished it, you may decide to ditch your broker, or at least ask him or her some very tough questions. You may decide to seek out an advisor anew, determined to look past superficial traits and slick sales pitches for the substance that this book will teach you to understand and expect.

Or you may decide to forego using an advisor, and manage your investment portfolio yourself. As I explain in detail in Chapter 7, investing is not all that difficult if you follow a disciplined process.

Over the years, I have learned that regardless of the route that consumers choose to reach their financial goals, their success or failure often hinges on their own makeup as much as anything. With that in mind, I've devoted a significant chunk of the book to helping you understand the emotions and mental machinery that can trip you up in everything from investing your own money to choosing an advisor. It's my hope and belief that understanding our internal workings as human beings can help us to make more rational, and ultimately wiser, decisions.

I flatter myself that many readers will find this book entertaining. Seeing how Wall Street works is, after all, a pretty juicy subject. But if the book does no more than feed cynicism about Wall Street, it will have failed. Because the takeaway should not be that *we're all screwed* and that it's impossible to find a good advisor. It should be the opposite: that even though Wall Street may see you as a sheep to be sheared, you're not a sheep. You are a consumer—and as all salesmen know, **the customer is *always* right**.

Consumers have serious power. As individuals, they have the power to protect their interests by choosing wisely. As a group, they just may have the power to do what lawmakers and regulators seem unable to do: Through exercising the power of choice, and backing it with the power of their wallets, consumers can change the very way that the financial advisory industry operates.

Steven D. Lockshin

Chapter 1

Is This Any Way to Choose an Advisor?

Imagine that you're on a hospital gurney, having just been wheeled into an operating room to undergo surgery to remove a brain tumor. You're understandably anxious. Your surgeon appears and greets you. Everything about him inspires confidence, from his impeccable credentials to his confident demeanor, right down to his square jaw. He's your man. Your surgeon seems to have come straight from central casting, and you experience a wave of comfort.

Just as the anesthesiologist adds a sedative to your IV, you notice something strange. Your surgeon's scrubs are covered with patches of major company names—patches just like those that NASCAR drivers wear to promote their sponsor companies. Instead of the logos for Pennzoil or Walmart, though, your surgeon's patches bear the logos of corporations in the medical field—device makers, pharmaceutical companies, even insurance companies.

... this surgery is brought to you by my sponsors ...

The anesthesiologist just asked you to start counting backward from 10, but your mind is racing with unsettling questions: Is this surgeon focused on his sponsors or me? Will every choice that he makes during the next several hours be based purely on improving my odds of survival? Or is there a chance that he will choose one drug or device over another just because a certain pharmaceutical or device company cut a sponsorship deal with his practice? Might he use surgical instruments that are second-rate? Might he even cut corners to please the insurance company, lining his pockets in the process or in order to earn his right to attend the next Hawaiian boondoggle?

Then, just as you lose consciousness, you feel a flashing sense of betrayal: *Why were you not told that your surgeon answers to corporate sponsors?* He should answer to his patients only, and his focus should be on saving lives—period. He shouldn't have even the slightest appearance or thought of a conflict of interest. And if those potential conflicts of interest do exist; they damned well shouldn't be hidden until it's too impractical to change surgeons.

Bad Financial Medicine

Luckily for all of us, this kind of scenario is pure fantasy. Sure, medicine has its flaws like every profession. But surgeons certainly aren't known for putting their patients' lives at risk for a few extra bucks.

If only the financial advice industry were the same. In survey after survey, Americans report that their financial health is their second highest priority, just behind the importance of their physical health. And yet the industry that Americans turn to for advice about how to manage their wealth, safeguard it, and pass it on to their loved ones is predominantly riddled with conflicts of interest.

In fact, I'd say that the financial advice industry has more built-in conflicts of interest than almost any other industry. I should know—I've been in the industry for more than 20 years and I founded one of the largest independent financial advice firms in the country, catering to some of the world's wealthiest families. Based on my experience, I can assure you that a huge percentage of financial advisors live in a world where doing the right thing for the customer is usually *not* the most common course of action.

Sadly, most people have no idea that's the case. If Americans knew how the industry works, they would be far more selective in choosing advisors. By the time you finish reading this book, you'll understand just how conflicted the financial services industry is.

You'll also find out how you can bypass most, if not all, of the conflicted advisors and find the ones that work purely in your interests—and yes, they're out there. You may even find out that managing your own investments is the best route for you.

Here's a simple example of a pervasive conflict of interest in the financial advice industry. Let's say your advisor is affiliated with one of the big, prestigious Wall Street firms. He's decided that your investment portfolio should include a mutual fund that invests in international companies. He recommends a fund to you and explains the reasoning for the investment, and you give him the green light to buy shares of that fund for your account.

Perhaps what your advisor didn't tell you is that the mutual fund he just recommended carries a higher sales fee than several other appropriate funds. The sales fee comes right out of your account and typically goes right into the broker's pocket—a simple but clear conflict of interest. Perhaps he didn't tell you that his firm receives a fee—more colorfully called a *kickback*— for having that fund on its menu of investment options (the industry calls this *paying for shelf space*).

The advisor hasn't violated any laws. Although he calls himself an advisor—a term that suggests he's in the business of giving objective advice—technically he's a broker. And, since brokers are typically paid some form of commission, they are, in effect, salesmen. According to the law, brokers can sell you any product that's deemed "suitable" for your needs. Now, that international mutual fund that was suggested was indeed suitable: It made your portfolio more diversified, which in theory will bolster your overall investment performance and/or reduce risk. What that broker didn't tell you is that several other mutual funds of the same type were suitable, too— and they might have cost significantly less. In fact, the funds your broker passed over may have not only been less expensive, but also better managed than the one he recommended. Again, your broker has not broken the law. In fact, brokers have no duty to tell their clients that better funds are available.

Trust me, this sort of conflict of interest plays out all the time in the brokerage business. It is the rule, not the exception. The majority of the industry is set up to push advisors into making decisions that put their interests ahead of those of their customers. Even advisors who want to do the right thing are prone to make the wrong decision and then rationalize that decision. They're human, after all, and humans are extremely good at talking themselves into decisions that make them money. And make no mistake, advisors' tainted decisions, added up over time, can make those advisors big money. The problem is that the consumer typically pays the price.

As a consumer, this dynamic can make reaching your long-term financial goals far more difficult than necessary. For one thing, paying unnecessarily high fees creates a tremendous drag on returns as investors try to reach their goals. In addition, conflicted investment advice often leads to poor performance. Conflicted advice is a problem for all consumers, from the working class to the very wealthy. It endangers everything from clients' standard of living to the amount of money they'll leave to their heirs or to charity.

A Murky Industry

Perhaps the world of financial advisors should be more like the world of NASCAR. Sure, sponsor emblems on advisors' suits may sound ridiculous, but at least that would tell consumers exactly where advisors' loyalties lie. It would be a welcome change to an industry that is not only highly conflicted but is also notorious for its lack of transparency.

Conflicts of interest, such as those involving sales fees, are only one murky part of the industry. There's a whole raft of important information that advisors simply don't have to disclose. And the information that regulators do require advisors to reveal is usually buried within long documents written in impenetrable legalese. The bottom line is that instead of providing consumers with truly useful information, the industry buries the information under a ton of irrelevant and confusing information.

An easy illustration of perplexing legalese is the ADV, the main disclosure form that SEC-registered advisors are required to produce. And these are supposed to be the good guys! If you think the disclosures will explain in plain English, as they're supposed to, whether an advisor has a consumer-friendly business model: Think again.

To me, advisors' disclosure forms are all about covering their asses, period. The typical disclosure form reminds me of those pages of tiny boilerplate print that accompany drug ads in magazines. No consumer can understand the technical mumbo jumbo—and the reality is that it's not written to be understood. Pharmaceutical companies publish the disclosures because, first, they're required to by the government, and second, because they serve as a shield against potential lawsuits. In the same way, the legal nonsense that passes for "disclosure" in the financial advice industry exists to protect advisors and product producers, not to inform consumers.

And the fact that Americans lack the clear, straightforward information by which they might evaluate their advisors is really bad news. It means the people that we as consumers turn to for advice on the critical subject of financial success can operate largely in the dark, putting their interests ahead of our own and hiding behind perplexing "disclosures." The perpetrators include advisors affiliated with well-regarded Wall Street firms or banks—in fact, as I'll explain later in the book, they're typically the worst offenders—as well as the smaller guys scattered throughout the system.

The confusing, consumer-unfriendly system that's in place means we don't know when an advisor is steering us to a certain investment just to collect a higher sales fee. It means we don't know when Wall Street firms are pushing our advisor to sell complex, expensive products mainly designed to make those firms—and those firms' shareholders—a bundle at our expense. It means we have no simple way to tell whether our financial advisor is truly on our side.

But the problems with the system don't end there. When consumers choose a financial advisor, they almost always do so without critical information about the very viability of the advisor's business.

Does the advisor who wants to manage your wealth have a large enough client base to succeed? Is her practice properly insured? Does he have a solid succession plan so that his clients won't be stranded in the event of his untimely death? Will her firm keep your assets at an independent, third-party custodian, or will it hold them in-house—the arrangement that allowed Bernie Madoff to perpetrate his Ponzi scheme?

This is just a sample of the basic, factual information that should always be used when choosing an advisor. It's the equivalent of knowing the model, gas mileage, and warranty terms before buying a car. Yet clear information about advisors is a mystery to investors. In fact, most consumers don't even *know what they need to know* in order to choose a financial advisor. So they end up selecting advisors in a way that makes little sense, and is in fact dangerous to their financial wellbeing. And, mind you, none of these topics touch on the fees and where they are clear versus buried in mysterious structures or small print.

"You Should Meet My Guy"

Let's go back to medicine for a moment, and imagine another high-stakes scenario. Suppose your spouse or your child or another person you care deeply about is diagnosed with that life-threatening brain tumor suggested earlier. You learn that tumors of this sort can be successfully removed, but that the procedure is extremely sensitive—brain damage or even death on the operating table are very real possibilities.

You need to choose a surgeon. How do you proceed? Do you simply go to the local hospital? Do you ask your friends if they or their friends know of a brain surgeon they "like"? Do you choose the most handsome doctor? How about one that took you to the Knicks game courtside? Of course not. You do some serious research when making a decision of this magnitude.

You find independent rankings of the best medical centers and best surgeons. You research each doctor's education and experience. You investigate their surgery outcomes. You check their backgrounds for cases of malpractice. You use every single resource at your disposal. You are as thorough as you can possibly be.

It's hard to conceive of someone putting their loved one's fate in the hands of a doctor based on an advertisement or a recommendation from the friend of a friend. Yet *this is exactly how consumers select financial advisors.*

Financial advisors, including me, get the vast majority of their new clients through referrals from existing clients. Some advisors are shrewd marketers, and the most savvy have built huge businesses through well-funded advertising or even direct-mail campaigns.

Once an advisor gets to meet with a person who's been drawn in by a referral or an advertisement, it's very easy to turn that person into a client. Any successful advisor knows that, once a prospect is sitting across from them, it's like shooting fish in a barrel. At the point of sale, the universe of choices for the investor is typically reduced to a few recommended advisors and, most often, it's the best salesman that wins. It's pretty much a personality contest.

It's implied that advisors almost always know more about investing, estate planning, and other financial matters than their prospective clients do. So once they start spouting facts and figures with confidence,their position as an authority figure is quickly established.

Looking like an advisor doesn't hurt, either. There's a reason for dark suits and a clean, buffed complexion—advisors dress to make an impression.

Closing the deal is typically a function of salesmanship. The trick, as any salesperson worth his salt knows, is to get the prospective customer to start agreeing with him or her. "I assume you want to protect your lifestyle." Yes, of course—the prospect nods his head. "Do you want the minimum-risk portfolio required to meet your objectives?" More nodding. "Do you want to be able to pass on as much of your wealth as possible to your loved ones rather than to Uncle Sam?" More enthusiastic agreement—the prospective customer starts to think: *This guy really understands me!* In fact, no one in their right mind would answer "no" to these sorts of questions—which is precisely why the advisor asks them. Once an advisor gets you nodding your head, you're on your way to being their client.

More often, the wealthiest families exercise a little more diligence. They may interview multiple advisors and choose the one that most impresses them. But the dynamic is the same: They almost always choose the advisor who makes the best impression, the one who's the most persuasive. In other words, they choose the best salesman. It's as simple as that.

You'd think that potential clients really grill me and other financial advisors before entrusting us with their fortunes. In fact, they often don't know the right questions to ask. They ask "softball" questions about how we invest, how we'll make them money and protect their capital. Because these questions are open-ended and based on emotion rather than facts, it's easy to tell clients exactly what they want to hear.

"How can you protect me from another market crash?" a client might ask—that's their fear talking. "Can you make me more money than the other guy?" another might ask—a question rooted in greed. "I'm conservative. I don't want to lose money." (I still haven't had a prospect come in and say, "I want to lose money." And I'm not holding my breath.) Most advisors are very good at persuading potential clients that they can successfully steer them through a market crash or beat the market. The truth is that most believe it, and their sincerity in conveying that belief to potential new clients is a big reason that those "prospects" so often become clients. Few advisors are able to understand their own limitations, and fewer still are professional enough to acknowledge them.

What should truly matter to consumers is not whether an advisor seems sincere. Rather, their focus should be on whether an advisor has the goods to deliver solid advice, performance, and service. Finding that out requires consumers to ask for quantifiable, factual information. But they rarely do. I'm almost never asked detailed questions about how I'm paid and how much my services cost. Rarely am I asked whether I am legally bound to put clients' interests first and foremost. (Legalese for this desirable behavior is "acting as a fiduciary.")

Potential clients too often fail to ask me or my peers the factual, non-emotional questions such as where their assets will be custodied, whether our businesses are large enough to survive major turmoil, and what would happen if you or I were to die suddenly.

I wince when I think of how typical consumers "vet" advisors because I know that it makes them vulnerable not only to second-rate advisors but to outright crooks. Bernie Madoff's Ponzi scheme absolutely wiped out client after client after client, costing those who trusted him $65 billion in all (including fictitious gains that people believed they had actually earned). Most, if not all, of these folks were wealthy and sophisticated. I know a number of them. Investors flocked to Madoff because what he offered answered their emotional needs. He provided little information, just enough to entice the greedy instinct of his victims to engage. Many investors simply reassured themselves with thoughts such as, "Well, if it's good enough for [*insert rich person's name*], then it's good enough for me." The relatively high returns appealed to investors' greed, and the year-in-year-out consistency of those returns answered the universal fear of market sell-offs.

Madoff was a smooth, masterful salesman selling irresistible—even a little too good to be true—results. But one simple, fact-based question would have ruled out Madoff as a prospective advisor: "Do you keep your clients' assets with an independent, third-party custodian?" Madoff did not, of course—he kept clients' assets in his company's own account, and used them to pay fictional returns to other clients. Asking that question and heeding the answer could have prevented Madoff's clients against the destruction that he wrought.

Why is it that people who would leave no stone unturned in researching a surgeon to protect their health, or even doing extensive research before purchasing a new car, are so incredibly cavalier in selecting an advisor to manage their financial wealth? Choosing the wrong financial advisor can dramatically alter your future and the future of your family. At the very least, consumers should be more rigorous in evaluating advisors because they pay those advisors very well to look after their interests.

But while consumers definitely need to take the process of selecting an advisor more seriously, they're not the only ones to blame. The industry and regulators together have created, and are maintaining, an environment where conflicts of interest are built in—and hidden. And together they've created a status quo in which it's impossible to distinguish the advisors you should avoid from those who deserve your business.

Key Points

- The majority of the financial service providers are conflicted.
- While the significant majority of "financial advisors" are conflicted and economic conflict often gets in the way of good advice, there are many good advisors out there who truly put their clients' interests first.
- With some simple tools and some discipline, you can separate the true "fiduciary" advisors from the folks who may have ulterior motives.

- Consumers don't know what they don't know.
- The first tool in the arsenal of "product pushers" is *small print* and confusing language.
- All advisors are conflicted when trying to make the sale. However, once you hire a fee-only advisor, that conflict can be reduced or eliminated.
- Sadly, the industry has stacked the odds against consumers, despite their objections—and claims—to the contrary.

Chapter 2

Wall Street's Dirty Secrets

I f you've ever seen movies about the brokerage world—think *Wall Street* or *The Boiler Room*—you know there's a formula: A naïve, young broker enters the industry and quickly finds out just how cynical and ugly it is.

That's pretty much my story. I started in the advisor business 26 years ago, as a 19-year-old intern at a regional brokerage firm. The senior brokers would always answer my questions honestly and directly. I recall that one day I asked one of the top producers how he decided which investments to put in a client's portfolio.

I'll never forget his answer. While he always protected his clients with a base of quality municipal bonds, the choice for the balance of the portfolio had different criteria. "If there are two products and they're both decent—and who really knows which will perform better?" he told me, "I'll always select the one that pays me more."

In other words, he would stick his customers with higher fees in order to enrich himself. He was able to rationalize away the conflict by supposing that it was impossible to know which choice would perform best in the future. Common sense, however, would dictate that since fees are a significant component of investment returns, my teacher was hurting his clients' investment results even as he helped himself. Vanguard, the largest mutual fund company in the world and creator of index investing, highlights data supporting the impact of fees on their website (see the following sidebar).

In a February 2002 study, the Financial Research Corporation evaluated the predictive value on future performance of 10 different metrics, including past performance, Morningstar ratings, alpha, and beta. In their study, expense ratios were the most reliable predictor of future performance, with low-cost funds delivering above-average performance in all of the periods examined.[1] Likewise in a 2004 Lipper Research Study, Clark investigated how well expenses and net returns predict future mutual fund performance. Clark found that for no-load equity and no-load bond mutual funds, the lowest expense quintile produced more index-beating funds than any other expense quintile.[2]

[1]Financial Research Corporation, "Predicting Mutual Fund Performance II: After the Bear," Boston, 2002.
[2]Andrew Clark, "How Well Do Expenses and Net Returns Predict Future Performance?" Lipper Research Study (May 2004), www.lipperweb.com/research/searchResults.asp.

The broker referenced above is not a bad guy, nor is he a bad advisor. However, he could have done better for his clients were it not for the allure of differentiated compensation.

Even back then, the brokerage industry portrayed itself as the ally of the client. Remember the commercial catchphrase, "When E.F. Hutton Talks, People Listen"? Stockbrokers were supposed to be the guys who gave you valuable information; they were your Sherpas as you climbed the mountain of wealth.

In fact, that image has always been baloney. Brokerage firms have always been commission-oriented, which means they have always been sales-oriented. And, this means they've never acted purely in the clients' best interests.

Back at the brokerage firm where I interned and then started my career, lists of the top-earning brokers were prominently posted each day, and everyone in the office knew who the big dogs were. The company made sure the big dogs got their recognition, because, of course, the company got a cut of the commissions. That's how it works in any sales organization.

At this brokerage firm (and likely in all of the others), the culture was macho, competitive and profit-driven, and that meant that clients were often the losers. This company definitely didn't rank how well the brokers actually helped clients succeed; that was beside the point.

You might think that in the quarter-century that's passed since then, the brokerage industry's culture must have changed. In fact, it's astonishing how little it's changed. Sure, these firms have improved their image: "Brokers" have now become "advisors" or "wealth counselors," and advertisements have been tailored to imply that the industry is on your side.

And based on the amount of assets Wall Street manages, consumers are still buying the marketing pitch. I submit that they're buying an illusion. Although it dresses up its focus on sales with advice, the typical brokerage firm earns the majority of its money by pushing products that are better for the firm than for its clients. The product manufacturers may pay the firms or it may come directly in the form of a fee or commission, but one thing is certain— it comes out of the investors' end of the deal.

The More Things Change . . .

The front-page headline in the July 2, 2012, issue of the *New York Times* tells the story. Written in

2012, it could just as easily have appeared 20 or 30 years ago:

The New York Times

Former Brokers Say JPMorgan Favored
Selling Bank's Own Funds Over Others

Matt Corrado © 2013

Competing Priorities (client needs versus a paycheck!)

In short, the article explained that JPMorgan encouraged its brokers to push expensive investment products that it had created in-house, and suggested a simple reason—to help it prop up profits in the wake of the financial crisis.

Financial advisors at JPMorgan told the *Times*: "They were encouraged, at times, to favor JPMorgan's own products even when competitors had better-performing or cheaper options." In one case, the *Times* reported, JPMorgan's marketing materials even exaggerated the returns of the mutual funds the company was managing and selling.

JPMorgan has had a high-class image. But the *Times* story suggests an environment that's not very far removed from a boiler-room culture where investments are pushed onto overly trusting customers. After one JPMorgan advisor had successfully steered a client to invest $75,000 in an in-house mutual fund, a supervisor responded with an e-mail including the subject line: "KABOOM." "Nice to know someone is taking advantage of the best selling day of the week," the supervisor wrote.

One former JPMorgan broker told the *Times* that if he did not persuade a customer to invest in an expensive in-house product, his manager would badger him as to why he had selected something else. "It was all about the money, not the client," the broker said.

To give you an idea of how entrenched the sales culture is on Wall Street, consider that the events that the *Times* reported in this story occurred just one year after JPMorgan had been forced to pay a $373 million fine. The reason for the fine—JPMorgan was punished for pushing its own investment funds despite having agreed to sell alternative funds from an outside manager.

The big dogs of the investment sales game are still held up as shining examples for their comrades. The same *Times* article revealed that JPMorgan "circulates a list of brokers whose clients collectively have . . . the largest amounts in the Chase Strategic Portfolio." This is exactly the kind of thing that I'd witnessed early in my career. More than 20 years later, things have barely changed.

So, why does this entrenched sales culture matter to you? It's not just that the extra fees that the brokerages pocket come out of your savings and investments. It's not only because the products they recommend may not be as good as the alternatives. It's because when your advisor works within such a culture, you can't trust that he or she is on your side—and, because these brokers are human, they often can't trust themselves to choose well while their primal emotions of greed and fear kick in.

What's the *Rap* on Wrap Programs?

Over the years, Wall Street has made well-publicized efforts to bolster clients' impressions that they are being treated fairly. Broker-ages that typically sold their own products now boast of "open architecture," usurping the language used by true open-architecture firms. "Open architecture" is in effect when a firm's customers can access the majority of the universe of mutual funds, hedge funds, and other products managed outside the firm by independent third parties. In my view, it's debatable whether brokerage firms can be said to offer open architecture. Size constraints, payment arrangements, and proprietary products are all challenges that restrict the universe of choices.

Wall Street's big firms also tout alternatives to their traditional commission model, including mutual fund "wrap" accounts. Through wrap accounts, customers can choose from a large selection of investment managers while paying a single annual fee—typically around 1 percent or higher of assets invested in the account. The fee replaces the sales commission that customers would otherwise pay their broker each time they bought or sold shares of stocks or a fund.

In theory, wrap accounts eliminate the temptation for advisors to recommend funds based on the commissions they pay. But even a product like a wrap account involves a conflict of interest for brokers. Since the brokerage's 1 percent fee is fixed, the firm and the broker can increase their profits by narrowing the universe of choices to lower-cost providers. And low-cost providers in these programs are not necessarily the best providers. Often they are the firms willing to cut deals in order to pay for distribution.

"You Don't Understand . . . "

Wall Street's culture has always been about selling stocks and bonds and earning commissions. That's why its firms are called "broker-dealers." Brokerages like to talk about how they give advice, but advice doesn't make them money. Selling a product does. Brokerages don't just have an incentive to sell products: No matter how much they try to muddy the issue, selling products *is* their business model.

In recent years, consumers have started to catch on. So brokerages have simply changed the semantics— "brokers," you'll remember, are now "advisors"—but, for the most part, they haven't changed their culture. If anything, the pressure to sell products is stronger than ever.

One reason is their corporate structure. Brokerage firms that were traditionally privately owned partnerships are today publicly traded companies or parts of publicly traded companies. Their focus, more than ever, is on generating rising profits, quarter after quarter, to please their investors. Ironically, *Wall Street is pushing for profits to please Wall Street analysts.*

Pleasing their investors drives up the companies' stock prices, which further enriches executives whose compensation includes huge chunks of their firms' stock and stock options.

Furthermore, rules that once kept banks, brokerages, and other kinds of financial companies separate are long gone. When Congress abolished the Depression-era Glass-Steagall Act back in 1999, Wall Street executives were ecstatic. The door had opened to selling customers more and more products and reaping ever-larger profits.

The result was sprawling, profit-hungry corporations like CitiGroup. When financial-industry legend Sandy Weill created CitiGroup in 1998 by combining financial conglomerate Travelers Group with Citicorp, the culture at the latter changed abruptly.

John Reed, the CEO and chairman of Citicorp in the 1980s and 1990s, described the change in a recent interview:

I never heard of shareholder value until the 1990s. It was *customers, customers, customers.* How are the customers? Are we doing well or are we losing place with the customers and all of a sudden, Sandy was a total proponent, Sandy Weill, his whole life was to accumulate money. He said, "John, we could be so rich." Being rich never crossed my mind as an objective. I was almost embarrassed that somebody would say it out loud. . . . The biggest bonus I had ever received when I was at Citi was $3 million. The first year I worked with Sandy (as co-CEO) it was $15 million. I said to the Board, 'I am the same guy doing the same job, at the same company, the company is bigger, but there are two of us. What is going on?'

They said, "You don't understand."

In recent years, Wall Street "wirehouses"—the big brokerage firms like Morgan Stanley, Merrill Lynch, UBS, and Smith Barney have made their focus on profits even clearer. These firms have been forcing brokers who generate revenue of less than $400,000 or $500,000 per year to leave the company—while dangling handsome bonuses in order to lure away the biggest, cash-cow brokerage teams from their rivals. In fact, the primary driver for brokers changing firms is not for better tools to serve you; it's for a bigger payday. That's so much the case that the brokerage industry's regulator, the Financial Industry Regulatory Authority (FINRA), has considered making brokers disclose their recruitment bonuses to clients. The concern is that brokers may be tempted to push unnecessary sales on clients in order to meet their production and asset targets specified in their recruitment packages.

The cynical side of me says that if the requirement is put in place—and that's a big *if*—the disclosures will be as difficult to find and understand as all of the other disclosures currently required of financial advisors.

The focus on profits by Wall Street and the financial industry in general has been wildly successful. In 2010, just a few years after the financial crisis that caused many of these institutions to accept government bailouts, financial services only accounted for about 8 percent of the U.S. gross domestic product—but more than 29 percent of U.S. GDP profits, according to the *Wall Street Journal*. This number was closer to 40 percent prior to the financial crisis and as high as 46 percent in 2001. Simply put, these profits arrived predominantly on the backs of consumers.

To their credit, the big Wall Street firms no longer try to deny that their companies' profits are their first priority. In the midst of JPMorgan's "Whale of London" debacle, which likely cost shareholders an amount in excess of $6 billion, CEO Jamie Dimon vowed to manage the loss *"to maximize economic value for shareholders."*

Misplaced Interests

The core reason that consumers should be wary of brokerage firms is their conflicts of interest. Conflicts are built into the industry's business model. But what really enables brokers and their companies to act in ways that hurt investors is the weak regulatory standard under which they operate.

Brokers are regulated by the Financial Industry Regulatory Authority (FINRA), a self-regulating organization (imagine prisoners running the prison). FINRA regulates brokers under what's known as the "suitability standard." The suitability standard is nothing less than a license to sell investors products that might not serve their best interests.

The "standard" is what allows people like the brokers at my old firm to recommend product A to his clients rather than product B, which is less costly and maybe even better in quality. It's more or less a legal cover for unethical behavior.

The great news for consumers is that there's a second advisor standard out there—the fiduciary standard. The fiduciary standard requires your advisor to act in your best interests, period. This standard, however, is governed by the Securities and Exchange

Commission (SEC), not FINRA, and it only applies to advisors they have jurisdiction over. If the brokers at the firm where I was an intern at adhered to the fiduciary standard, the broker I mentioned would have answered my question regarding how he decided which investments to put in a client's portfolio like this: "If there are two products to choose from and they're both similar and appropriate, I'll always select the one that costs the client less."

An advisor under the fiduciary standard is legally bound to do what's best for you in every situation. If he sells you a more expensive product when an alternative is available, he will have broken the law and can be held accountable by the SEC.[3] All financial advisors understand that the fiduciary standard is much more rigorous than the suitability standard.

Unfortunately, most investors don't understand the components of what constitutes a true fiduciary. Many aren't even familiar with the term. The answer lies in a plethora of legal descriptions that would make most individuals glaze over after a few sentences.

---

[3]The Securities and Exchange Commission regulates all Registered Investment Advisors with over $100 million under management as well as certain other RIAs.

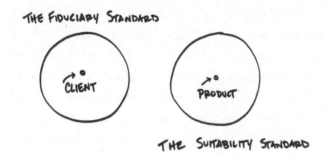

Most Wall Street brokers are subject only to the suitability standard. Thankfully for consumers, there's a whole category of advisors—known as registered investment advisors (RIAs)—who have chosen to be bound by the more stringent fiduciary standard. They're known as RIAs or, more typically Independent Advisors, and their ranks are growing. You'll learn more about RIAs a bit further on in this book.

Brokers and Advisors

Remember my tongue-in-cheek suggestion that advisors should be made to wear sponsor patches in order to make plain their conflicts of interest? Here's another pie-in-the-sky suggestion that would greatly benefit consumers and this alone could completely tilt the industry in favor of the consumer: **Individuals and companies who provide unconflicted financial advice should be allowed to call themselves "advisors," while those who operate under conflicts of interest should be required to call themselves "brokers."**

We'd all understand "advisors" to be objective and on the consumer's side, and we'd understand "brokers" to be what they often are: salespeople, who may be on your side or likely may not be. This system would make it so much easier to find someone to help us with investments and other financial matters. What's more, it would stop the nauseating practice of brokers—the salespeople—describing themselves as "consultants," "investment counselors," and "investment advisors" in order to mislead consumers.

Unfortunately, this system isn't really workable. Advisors and brokers can't always be neatly categorized. There are plenty of "advisors" who have figured out how to game the system so that their interests come before clients'. You'll learn more about that ugly practice later in the book. Moreover, there are plenty of exceptional brokers, folks who "do the right thing." The problem is that it's nearly impossible to tell one from the other.

For now though, it's useful to oversimplify a bit and think of the financial advice industry as being divided into two camps. One camp consists of independent advisors who provide conflict-free advice. These advisors, who have been rapidly growing in numbers in recent years, adhere to the consumer-friendly set of rules known as the fiduciary standard (again, there are plenty of bad apples in this bunch). The other camp consists of brokers, who operate under the salesman-friendly set of rules known as the suitability standard. These brokers belong to the old, entrenched, and consumer-*un*friendly culture I refer to, very simply, as Wall Street (there are some good advisors here, but their environment is a powerful aphrodisiac when it comes to conflicts of interest).

Wall Street Brokers versus Main Street Consumers

There's little question among knowledgeable people that the fiduciary rules are better for consumers than the rules that are applied to brokers. It came as little surprise then, that in the wake of the 2008 market crash, lawmakers seeking to protect consumers from further setbacks set out to extend the fiduciary standard to the brokerage industry. What happened next was, likewise, no surprise.

The brokerage industry fought the effort as if its life depended on it—which it probably does. Its trade group, SIFMA,[4] along with the insurance industry, trained their lobbying cannons on Congress in an effort to stop the rule change. Their Orwellian argument was that the fiduciary standard would hurt consumers by increasing costs, reducing choices, and putting the valuable services of a broker out of reach for many. Little mentioned was the fact that it might also diminish the industry's profits.

Finally, three years after the fiduciary standard was proposed, SIFMA seemed to change course and embrace a uniform standard for *all* brokers and advisors. SIFMA probably had little choice given the broad support for the more consumer-friendly standard. Still, the industry's about-face was a sham. The uniform fiduciary standard it endorsed was its own

---

[4]The Securities Industry and Financial Markets Association (SIFMA) represents hundreds of the largest securities firms, banks, and asset managers.

warped version, which closely resembled the traditional broker suitability standard. Rather than raising the bar to the SEC standard, SIFMA suggested lowering all standards to their level.

Peddling Products

You might think that Wall Street's business is investing, but to a large extent, Wall Street's business is psychology. The product development teams at the major financial institutions—places like Merrill Lynch, Morgan Stanley, JPMorgan, and UBS—are impressive students of human psychology. They deftly create complex products that play to investors' craving for big returns with little risk.

As you might guess, the products are extremely profitable for the firms that create them. They're often less so for investors.

Look at a product like collateralized debt obligations (CDOs). CDOs are complex securities—essentially packages stuffed with bonds, loans, and other assets. CDOs, including those that contained very risky mortgages, became more and more popular in the first few years of the 2000s. As a result of the subprime mortgage crisis that began in 2007, CDOs' values collapsed, leaving the investors who owned them with dramatic losses.

It's clear that a great many of the people involved in the disastrous CDO market just didn't understand the products—and that includes both the investors who bought them and the brokers who sold them. But what did that matter? CDOs were marketed to appeal to investors' basic emotions of fear and greed. They delivered returns that were higher than those of most bonds, but investors were told—erroneously— that they were a safe alternative to bonds. They were the proverbial "free lunch."

Dealers of these securities will argue that consumers demanded them and that their competitors were creating the same solutions, so why shouldn't they? While it's true that consumers demanded these high-yield, highly rated securities; giving in to consumer demands was the equivalent of allowing cocaine to be sold as medicine at your local pharmacy. Whose fault is the codependence? Is it the drug dealers' (product manufacturers)? Or the drug users' (the consumers)? Both were to blame. However, I submit that it's the pharmacists' (advisors') responsibility to prohibit this vicious circle. It's the advisors, after all, who should understand the potential damage from poorly thought-out solutions.

In selling these products to investors whether they understood them or not, Wall Street's brokers were just behaving as you'd expect a typical human in this culture to behave. Brokers want to sell products and their companies provide products that clients want. And the weak regulatory standard that brokers operate under means that they can recommend products like CDOs, even when the brokers don't understand whether these securities belong in clients' portfolios or not.

By the way, if you're worried by the idea of brokers who don't understand the products they're selling, you should know that the industry actually is full of smart and talented people. Unfortunately, most of them are not advisors. They're more likely to work in developing those irresistible products, or trading stocks and bonds for their companies' own accounts (something the 2010 Dodd-Frank Wall Street Reform and Consumer Protection Act has attempted to eliminate). Yes, there are talented investment advisors in the brokerage industry. But they're the exception. Most just aren't very good at doing their core job of managing client portfolios to meet client objectives.

I've believed for a long time that consumers would be much better off if they were all served by the fraction of really good, competent people in the industry. Unfortunately, just about anyone can enter the brokerage industry—or the advisory industry at large, for that matter. As you'll soon learn, the industry's barriers to entry and education requirements are almost nonexistent. As a member of the industry, I frankly find them embarrassing.

Omission versus Commission

Often it's not what brokers do wrong that hurts their clients—it's what they fail to do. For instance, advisors' jobs are really very simple when it comes to investing their clients' money. Most of the job is really just math and a little bit of judgment. An effective advisor should understand a client's goals and their time frame to meet those goals, determine the level of risk that the client is comfortable with, and then identify an investment portfolio at that intersection of goals and risk that will meet their client's objectives.

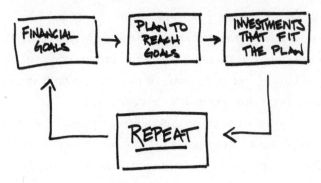

Over the years, advisors should regularly adjust the investment mix to make sure clients stay on track to reach their goals and that their portfolio remains balanced.

There's really no need for clients to load up on hot sectors—as many did prior to the dot-com crash in the early 2000s. There's little need for clients to include CDOs, derivatives, or other overly complicated products in their portfolios. But again and again, they do. Sometimes advisors push hot products. But other times it's their clients pushing to purchase them. In that situation, good advisors are supposed to push back—reminding clients that long-term success requires a diversified, balanced portfolio and that chasing returns via the *hot product du jour* is almost always a bad idea. Just think about two of the hottest initial public stock offerings of the decade: Facebook and Groupon. Investors clamored to get shares of the companies, but at the time of this writing both stocks have been disasters as IPO investments.

Too often advisors are well-paid *yes-men*: If their clients want hot products, who are they not to fill the order? And it's not just investments. How many advisors have urged their clients not to buy a house they really can't afford? To save more and consume less? To reduce their debt? Had they done so, the recession and market crash post-2008 might have been much less painful for countless people. When laymen are leveraging their life savings to purchase condos in Miami to *flip*, something is wrong—and too many advisors failed to intervene and instead act as voices of reason.

It takes a unique advisor to stand up to the pressures inherent to his or her position: pressure to earn more for themselves and their companies by selling higher-fee products; pressure from clients who want them to invest unwisely. Those unique advisors are out there, though. The challenge is to identify them—and as you'll learn, the power lies with consumers to do just that. Consumers can vote with their wallets for advisors who put clients' interests first and foremost and who have the skills to deliver great service. Remember, only consumers can require the industry to improve.

Key Points

- The more things change, the more they stay the same. Most brokers and bankers celebrate the success of commissions earned or products sold, not the quality of advice given.
- Public companies are focused on delivering shareholder value. In other words, on making their stock price go up. Most banks and brokerage firms are public companies.
- Conflicts of interest—situations where your advisor has to decide whether to put your needs ahead of his—are the key ingredient in the recipe for bad decision-making, and disclosure is not the antidote.
- Brokers and bankers regulated by FINRA are held to a lower "suitability standard," while Registered Investment Advisors regulated by

the SEC are held to a higher "fiduciary standard." Alas, this is not a panacea, since a loophole you can drive a Mack truck through exists—more on this later.

- Often it is a failure on an advisor's part to prohibit a bad decision that is worse than selling a bad product. "*Yes-men*" are dangerous collaborators with investor fear and greed.

Chapter 3

The Wall Street Whitewash

W all Street is not the only game in town for investors. Other options include banks, asset managers such as Fidelity Investments, Vanguard, and others, and registered investment advisors (RIAs). Among these categories, there is little question that *independent registered investment advisors* are the least conflicted option for investors. They are typically paid in a manner that minimizes or eliminates conflicts of interest, and they are legally required to operate under a stringent standard that places clients' interests ahead of their own. While we'll go into more depth on independent RIAs later, let's address the big names first.

Today, the majority of investors turn to Wall Street, a minefield full of conflicts of interest, exploitative products, and *yes-men*, to take care of the critical issue of their financial health. The traditional brokerage industry controls a staggering $5+ trillion of wealth from individuals, families, and institutions.

Is Wall Street concerned about its competitors? The answer has to be yes. In particular, it's been looking over its shoulder at the growing RIA industry. Since 2004, the number of RIAs has increased by 31 percent, to nearly 21,000, according to research firm Cerulli Associates. As of 2012, RIAs now control some $1.4 trillion of assets.

But independent registered investment advisors— those not affiliated with big brokerage companies or asset-management companies—are fighting an uphill battle. Most consumers don't even know independent advisors exist. A study by TD Ameritrade indicates that 84 percent of consumers don't know that independent advisors exist. Part of the reason for this is that independent advisors work as relatively small outfits rather than giant companies. The industry doesn't have the coordination and collective heft to raise its public profile through branding and marketing. And you should never underestimate the power of Wall Street's huge advertising budgets—or forget that, as their fee paying clients, you are paying for it!

Image Is Everything

One simple reason that Wall Street firms dominate the investment business is that they spend an obscene amount of cash promoting themselves through advertising. How much do they spend? To give you an idea, in 2010, Merrill Lynch's parent company, Bank of America, spent $1.9 billion on advertising. JPMorgan spent a staggering $2.4 billion, according to BusinessInsider.com.

Those companies didn't use all of that money to promote their brokerage arms and proprietary investment distribution, but you can be sure that they spent a healthy amount. And judging by their market share, those huge advertising budgets yield real results.

It's important to understand that advertisements from Wall Street brokerages don't have to persuade us that the companies offer the specific services we need. They don't have to prove that we'll get our money's worth. They don't have to talk about substance at all. They can be effective without any of that.

The truth is that successful advertising works on very simple psychological principles. It's as basic as making sure that the maximum amount of potential customers hear and see your name as frequently as possible, explains Professor Daniel Howard, a marketing professor at Southern Methodist University, in Dallas.

"Frequency—hearing and seeing a name like Merrill Lynch over and over again, on television, in magazines, on the web—has a powerful effect on consumer attitudes and beliefs," says Howard. "Simply put, we are comfortable with what we are familiar with. That is the essence of branding, and companies spend billions to associate their brand with what consumers desire."

"The frequency of hearing a company's name influences someone's familiarity," continues Howard. "And familiarity is primal in Homo sapiens in terms of feeling comfortable."

Daniel Kahneman, winner of a Nobel Prize in Economics, agrees. Here's what he had to say in his 2011 book, *Thinking, Fast and Slow*, about the power of repetition:

> A reliable way to make people believe in false-hoods is frequent repetition, because familiarity is not easily distinguished from truth. Authoritarian institutions and marketers have always known this fact.

So powerful is familiarity that studies have shown it's the strongest factor in predicting whether two people will become romantically involved, adds Howard. Familiarity with brands, he says, has the same power.

"And familiarity has the strongest impact in times of uncertainty," says Howard. "When someone is unsure what to buy, there is a strong and persistent tendency to pick the brand or company with which one is most familiar."

That means customers are likely to pick an advisor associated with a dominant brand like Merrill Lynch or UBS or Smith Barney in uncertain times, even though those companies were tainted by the financial crisis and stock market crash.

If frequency is one pillar of successful advertising, the other is having a broad geographic reach. A local RIA who gives her clients world-class service may be able to afford a bit of local advertising. But a broker for a huge Wall Street firm knows the name on his door is projected around the world day in and day out, year after year. He knows potential clients will be more inclined to trust him simply because the name of the company he represents registers deep in their subconscious.

Shopping Shortcuts

The pervasive advertising by Wall Street firms has been so successful that their company logos are very likely implanted deep in your mind—so deep you probably aren't even aware of it. Can you describe from memory the logo of Merrill Lynch? How about UBS? Citibank? Chase? Most likely you'd find it difficult—or maybe not very difficult—to give a good description of any one of their logos.

But it's also very likely that, shown any of the logos, not only would you recognize them immediately, but you would likely have a positive reaction. Robert Cialdini described the phenomenon of subconscious familiarity in his classic book on marketing, *Influence: The Psychology of Persuasion*.

"Often we don't realize that our attitude toward something has been influenced by the number of times we have been exposed to it in the past," he writes.

Cialdini cites an experiment in which faces of individuals were flashed on a screen so quickly that the subject of the experiment could not later recall having seen them. But the more times a person's face was flashed on the screen, the more the subject came to like that person—and trust their opinions—when the two eventually met in person.

Why does the brain act in this way? Cialdini and his peers suggest that humans have evolved to take shortcuts when making decisions. Kahnemann says these shortcuts are dictated by the "fast" brain. One shortcut is to trust those you know. Marketers for brokerages—and any other product or service— know this very well and use it in what Cialdini describes as "marketing jujitsu," using our own evolutionary adaptations to turn us into customers.

Another example of a shortcut we use has to do with a principle known as "social proof." In marketing terms, the principle of social proof means that a person is more willing to buy a product that he knows many other people have bought. Cialdini uses the example of toothpaste. An advertiser who informs us that a brand of toothpaste is selling faster or growing faster than all of its competing brands of toothpaste "has offered us valuable evidence about the quality of the product and the probability that we will like it," he writes.

In choosing which toothpaste to buy, we can either take a few days off from work to research every single brand, or we can trust that if the advertised brand is popular, it must be pretty good. "Four out of five dentists . . . " is an advertisement statement that many will recall. It's the sort of adaptation that has allowed the human race to make all of its incredible progress rather than being mired in endless, time-consuming, decision-making. The toothpaste shortcut "will likely steer us right, will unlikely steer us far wrong, and will conserve our cognitive energies for dealing with the rest of our increasingly information-laden, decision-overloaded environment," Cialdini writes.

When it comes to choosing a financial advisor, we are extremely inclined to take the toothpaste shortcut—that is, to rely on social proof. Almost all of my new clients come from referrals from existing clients, meaning those new clients use a version of the shortcut used by Cialdini's toothpaste shopper. Virtually every advisor I know in the industry, with a few notable exceptions, has built his or her client roster through referrals. It's effective, and quite frankly, independent "boutique" firms simply do not have the budget to build brand anyway.

But taking shortcuts in choosing an advisor is more dangerous than choosing the wrong toothpaste; in fact, it more closely resembles choosing the wrong surgeon. Our usual shortcut involves asking a friend, "Who's your guy?" And the person who is approached for a recommendation has usually found his advisor the same way. Client begets new client,

MY CIRCLE OF FRIENDS

you →●

who begets another new client. Or said differently, it's the uninformed steering the uninformed. Very rarely do new clients apply rigorous research to narrow down the field of advisors available to them. Bernie Madoff built a towering pyramid of customers this way.

There are too many advisors, and the differences between them are too hard to find and make sense of. So, we ask a friend we respect for a referral. Unfortunately, this is a terrible way to choose a steward for your investments and your financial affairs.

Facts versus Fluff

In recent years, brokerage firms' advertising budgets have had to do double duty. They've had the traditional job of keeping the company brand embedded in consumers' minds. But on top of that, they've been a means to try to repair these companies' images.

Some recent Merrill Lynch ads present a good case study. When Bank of America rolled out an ad campaign for Merrill Lynch

Wealth Management in June of 2012, it didn't talk about specific, verifiable information that would appeal to potential new clients.

Rather, its ads were full of intangibles and feel-good fluff. The company itself described the campaign's two television spots as "capturing the strength and optimism that the Merrill Lynch brand represents to clients and their advisors." Clients parsing the ads for how Merrill might prevent a repeat of the huge losses resulting from the 2008 financial crisis and market crash found nothing but fluff. There was certainly no mention of the fact that Merrill's poor judgment and greed had brought it to the brink of failure, and that only a shotgun marriage to Bank of America had saved it.

The cynicism of Wall Street's post-financial crisis advertising has been well documented in the press and the blogosphere. In 2010, Goldman Sachs launched a campaign that was clearly aimed at helping restore its image in the wake of the financial crisis. Over the previous months, Goldman's name had been dragged through the mud, notably in a famous *Rolling Stone* article in 2009, in which writer Matt Taibbi labeled the bank the "Vampire Squid" and accused it of helping to bring the financial system to the brink of ruin.

Goldman's print ads didn't talk about the wheeling and dealing that had helped bring the financial system to its knees. Instead they sought to polish the company's image by highlighting its more acceptable business activities. "How a plan to help a renewable energy company grow . . . Ended up creating more than just megawatts," read one typically self-congratulatory ad. The campaign's tagline: "Progress Is Everyone's Business."

Linda Kaplan Thaler, CEO of a Manhattan ad agency, told the *New York Times* the campaign "doesn't really get to the heart of how has this company changed in a way that I can find them trustworthy."

TheFinancialBrand.com blog dismissed the campaign with a simple question: "What does a wind farm, job creation, and 'progress' have to do with the myriad of black, nasty issues surrounding Goldman's bruised and battered brand?"

That's precisely the point, though. Such ads are almost never aimed at consumers' critical faculties. They're aimed at the lazy part of the brain. I'll explain what I mean in Chapter 7.

Vegas Rules

All gamblers know that the odds are stacked in favor of the house. They understand intellectually that, over time, they are far more likely to lose their money than to win. Yet legal gambling is staggeringly popular. In 2011 the top 20 U.S. casino markets earned combined annual revenue of $25.1 billion.

Think about that. The gaming industry manufactures nothing and provides no service beyond entertainment, and what's more, it's rigged against its customers, and everyone knows it. Yet the industry's U.S. revenues alone are nearly the size of Vermont's entire economy.

Matt Corrado © 2013

Retail investing can start to look a lot like Vegas.

Casinos have mastered the art of temptation and obfuscation—just like (you guessed it) Wall Street. Like the glitzy casinos in Las Vegas, Atlantic City, and elsewhere, the big brokerages spend lavishly on slick advertising to attract customers. You may be surprised to find that the similarities between the industries extend to their internal environments.

Play Money

Casinos bend our perceptions in order to disarm our critical abilities. The simple goal is to keep us wagering. A prime example is the conversion of money to the credits, tokens, and chips that are used in gambling. Using a stand-in for money makes the loss of actual money more abstract, and it makes us less likely to leave the poker table when we should.

Casinos' system of play money is not much different from what happens in the stock market. A good example has to do with companies that issue different classes of stock, each with a different price, or companies that "split" their stock. When a company splits its high-priced shares into twice as many shares, each valued at half its original price, investors will typically flock to buy those newly split shares. It doesn't matter that buying 200 shares of a stock today at $5 per share is the same as buying 100 shares at $10 each before the split. Investors react as if one gambling token had been turned into two. As the number of buyers increases, so does the stock price, but for no intelligent reason.

Disarming Complexity

Today's slot machines are extremely complex. Some machines allow gamblers to play dozens of lines at once, with varying bets on each. This complexity can overwhelm gamblers' critical faculties and quickly empty their wallets.

Wall Street is no different when it comes to product design. As in the gambling industry, there exists a barrage of psychological and financial incentives to lure consumers in until they can no longer take it or they come to their senses. This applies perfectly to the confusing "derivative" or "structured" products engineered to attract investors.

Mesmerizing Optics

Casinos aren't a great place to do rational thinking. Patrons' attention is dominated by shiny gambling equipment, video displays, and spinning wheels. The idea is to draw customers in and keep them drawn in—gambling and not reflecting.

The investing world is strikingly similar. Consider cable television channel CNBC, with its electronic ticker tape in perpetual motion, with the screen crowded by news updates and market data, with commentators shouting at you to buy this stock and sell that one. Think about our ever vibrating and ringing iPhones, BlackBerries, and other portable devices, all of them perfect for providing constant and immediate feedback on what should be long-term investments.

The VIP Racket

Casinos segment their customers according to their profitability. High-rollers are categorized within a "platinum" or "diamond" tier, for instance. And they enjoy fringe benefits such as access to supposedly more lucrative games.

Wall Street, too, uses a VIP system, with big investors granted access and privileges unavailable to the *small-fry* investor. Major Wall Street firms host lunches with former presidents and heads of state; they spoil customers with expensive golf and other trips. Just like the Vegas casinos that reserve cushy hotel suites for their *cash-cow* customers, Wall Street firms know that arranging exclusive events is an excellent investment. Ultimately, it's the customer

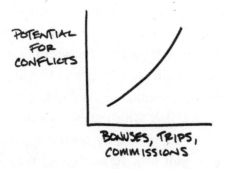

that pays the tab for his "privileged" relationship. Revenues from VIP clients are more than enough to cover the cost of exotic trips, insider dinners, and a hundred other amenities, with enough left over for the brokerage firm to pay itself handsomely.

Finally, the ways we react to Las Vegas and to Wall Street are similar, and that's due not to how those industries package their products but how we're wired internally.

Example: Whether we're in the stock market or at the roulette table, our losses loom larger than equal-sized gains. Research has shown that psychologically speaking, the pain of losing $100 is twice as great as the pleasure of winning $100. That phenomenon skews our decisions about when to take risk and when to play it safe.

When we approach investing as we do gambling, we may not be fully aware that we're doing so. But acting irrationally as an investor can be as ruinous as acting irrationally as a gambler. If you have the good fortune of winning at gambling, you may feel that you're "playing with the house's money," and thus have nothing to lose by continuing to gamble. Then, when your luck turns, you're likely to keep playing in an attempt to recover your losses.

This dynamic has played out countless times on casino floors all over the world, leading to remorse or worse. Unfortunately, investors have often felt the same as luckless gamblers, and for the same reasons.

Key Points

- Major Wall Street financial institutions benefit from branding built on billions of dollars of marketing budgets. Consumers provide the money for those budgets, perpetuating the brand.
- "A reliable way to make people believe in falsehoods is frequent repetition, because familiarity is not easily distinguished from truth. Authoritarian institutions and marketers have always known this fact." (Daniel Kahneman)
- When it comes to choosing a financial advisor, we are extremely inclined to take the *toothpaste shortcut*.
- Wall Street looks way too much like Las Vegas.

Chapter 4

Hold Your Nose: Other Advisor Options

I f you're over 50 years old, you probably remember when it used to be simple to buy a phone. Your choices were simple. Did you want the phone that hangs on the wall, or the one that sits on a table? Maybe you had to deliberate over color

. . . hmm, they all seem to look and smell the same . . .

choices: beige or black? Today's world still includes those old-fashioned landlines, but now you can choose from countless versions, including cordless phones. And of course, mobile phones and smartphones are available from a bevy of different manufacturers, with new products released continuously.

Phone shoppers now have to grapple with decisions that were unimaginable a couple of decades ago. What size screen do they want? Is it best to buy the current generation of a particular phone or wait a few weeks for the new version? Which operating system?

What about design and color? What kind of sleeve conveys the image the consumer wants to project? After all those decisions, today's phone buyers still aren't done: They have to choose a carrier and then a service plan for calls, texts, and data. It's almost enough to make you give up on phones completely, and perhaps use Skype or smoke signals as your phone—which is yet another choice.

Financial advice is no different. Once upon a time, if you had money to invest, you got in touch with a stockbroker. That broker recommended stocks and bonds, worked on commission, and was likely in the employ of one of the big, dominant Wall Street firms known as wirehouses.

Today, wirehouse brokers still dominate the world of financial advice. But they're no longer the only game in town. Like the telephone industry, the world of financial advice has become increasingly diverse. Yet choosing the right advisor is much more important than choosing the right phone. Advisors, after all, have a huge influence on your financial well-being. So it's worth your learning and understanding the differences between the categories of professionals who call themselves advisors.

Bank-Based Advisors

Many consumers' first impulse is to turn to their bank for investing guidance. They're already familiar with their bank, which engenders trust; they find it less intimidating than a brokerage house and, heck, they already do their banking there, so why not take care of two financial needs in one trip?

Banks, of course, welcome the additional business. For most of the twentieth century, commercial banks were legally shut out of the investment brokerage business. But after the Depression-era laws that prohibited them from selling investments were swept away in 1999, bank executives rushed to cash in. They set up what are known as retail brokerage businesses and began to "cross-sell" investments to their customers. At banks large and small, the key phrase is now "share of wallet." Customers with multiple products such as mortgages, life insurance, and investments are far more profitable than those with just bank accounts.

However your bank courts your investment business, though, there are good reasons to be skeptical:

- Working with a bank may seem somehow safer than other alternatives, but it's not. The FDIC insurance that covers your savings accounts, certificates of deposit, and other bank products does not apply to investments. It's no safer to buy stocks, bonds, mutual funds, life insurance policies, annuities, or municipal securities through a bank than it is to buy them elsewhere.

- Banks often have a more limited range of products than do other financial institutions.
- Bank-based advisors typically refer to themselves as "financial advisors" or "financial consultants." Don't be fooled by the semantics; most of the time, they're regular old brokers. They're salesmen, and they are subject to all the same conflicts as many brokers who work for Wall Street wirehouses.
- Advisors earn less at banks than they can at brokerage firms. That often results in shorter tenures as the better-skilled advisors leave for greener pastures. And when brokers leave banks, they typically cannot take their customers with them. That means the first broker you work with at a bank is unlikely to be your last.
- While sales skills are often the benchmark for success in acquiring clients, securing top intellectual

talent at banks is often difficult, as most banks pay relatively little in compensation. Top support staff, asset managers, and advisors most often find more fertile ground at other companies.

Private Banking and Trust Departments

Wealthier individuals and families often bypass banks' retail brokerages and turn to private banking departments to handle their investing, banking, borrowing, and other needs. Private bank clients enjoy more personal attention than retail bank customers, but the service they pay for is frequently rife with conflicts of interest. At issue is the temptation to use the bank's own investment managers rather than superior managers from outside the bank. In addition, the more products a private banking department can sell you, the more money the bank makes.

Edward Siedle, a former SEC attorney who is president of Benchmark Financial Services, made the case against private banking in a May 2010 column in Forbes.com:

> If you opt to let a private bank handle your affairs, you can expect your separately managed accounts to be filled with proprietary

products from the bank itself or from affiliated mutual funds, hedge funds, and money market funds.

This arrangement allows the bank to earn multiple layers of fees—often one for overseeing your overall portfolio and others for managing the sub-accounts. Such captive selling is highly entrenched. When a client who'd asked me to look into how her money was being managed asked her private bankers to invest in a hedge fund she'd become interested in on her own, she was told her relationship required that all her assets be invested in funds selected by the bank itself. Otherwise, of course, the bank risked cutting itself out of the fees that outside managers in such programs typically kick back to the bank.

Banks often do not fully disclose to clients "the potential harm such practices may do to their wealth," Siedle added.

Bank trust departments, which administer trusts and handle estate planning, are subject to conflicts of interest involving asset management, just as private banking units are. Bank trust departments often decide how to invest the assets within trusts, and if their institution has asset-management capabilities, they face the temptation to use in-house management even if better outside alternatives are available.

In addition to their conflicts of interest, bank trust departments rarely pass significant ownership to their key trust officers or compensate important relationship managers and other talent exceptionally well. This lack of ownership has, historically, engendered a revolving door phenomenon as trust officers move from institution to institution in an effort to further their careers.

Asset Managers

Companies that manage mutual funds and other investments—such as Fidelity Investments and Alliance Bernstein—have increasingly held themselves out as advisors, rather than distributors of their proprietary product. It's easy to understand why customers would be attracted to a well-known name such as Fidelity. But advisors who are directly affiliated with asset managers have a highly conflicted business model.

First of all, advisors who are affiliated with asset managers often lack the ability to recommend the best mutual funds and other investments for their clients. In some cases, the investment choices at their disposal are limited to those run by the company's asset-management arm—and a narrow product menu means that customers are probably not getting the best investments available in all categories, if even any categories. After all, no single firm has demonstrated exceptional ability in every type of investment.

Advisors at asset-management shops don't really have the freedom to be objective advice-givers. Objective advisors take their clients out of investments that perform poorly over time and reduce fees wherever possible, focusing almost exclusively on the result for the client. In contrast, when an advisor at Alliance Bernstein, Fidelity, or another asset manager sees that a client's portfolio of in-house investments is faring poorly, he's extremely unlikely—if not prohibited—from recommending that the client fire the firm. To properly serve their clients, advisors must be willing to fire poor asset managers. For advisors at asset-management companies, that would mean firing themselves. Bottom line: Their business involves a conflict of the highest order.

What's more, advisors who work for asset managers typically have an agenda beyond advising you, and that agenda is to make their employer as profitable as possible. No advisor in his right mind would share this fact with you. But the truth isn't hard to find. To find out what's expected of branch staff at Fidelity Investments' investor centers, just check out the company's recruiting site. The site states, quite frankly, that branch staff responsibilities include managing client accounts to "retain and increase total assets, revenues, and profitability." Staff is also expected to not only provide investment and financial planning guidance, but also to "cross-sell Fidelity products and services."

Insurance Salesmen

Top insurance brokers are adept at selling insurance. Many offer investments, too. Simply put, making an insurance sale is one of the more difficult sales of an intangible item. Discussing death—yours in particular—and spending money to buy something you will never enjoy just isn't a topic people wake up to each day and get excited about. Hence the old saying, "insurance is sold, not bought."

It would follow that if an insurance salesman can earn a consumer's trust—enough to buy insurance from him—then selling mutual funds or other securities shouldn't be too difficult. Why not earn some extra fees by doing so?

The challenge with this scenario is that selling insurance is one of the most conflicted sales there is. Chances are that your insurance agent is busy figuring out which of the insurance options he can sell you is most profitable for him. He's probably not focused on boning up on investment solutions or best practices for ensuring an outstanding customer outcome.

As with any of the professions or categories outlined in this book, there are practitioners who do care for their customer and, in the face of conflicted choices, often—if not always—do what's best for consumers. I believe, however, that when given a conflicted choice, most humans choose poorly. History would likely prove that premise to be true.

Fee-Only Planners

Almost diametrically opposed to the conflicted brokerage business model is the fee-only planner business model. Fee-only planners' business models ensure that they have little or no conflict of interest. They are fiduciaries, meaning that, unlike brokers, they must put their clients' interests before their own. They charge by the hour or by the project, usually in the $100- to $200-per-hour range, and are paid that rate no matter what they recommend.

All of that is great news for consumers. Customers of fee-only planners know that their advisor has no incentive to push any particular stock, bond, mutual fund, or other product. In my experience, fee-only advisors have absolutely the right motivation for being in the financial advisory business: to help their clients succeed—period. They're also more likely than brokers to have respected professional designations such as Certified Financial Planner (CFP), Certified Investment Management Analyst (CIMA), or Chartered Financial Analyst (CFA).

Because fee-only planners have no agenda beyond giving good advice, they're usually available for as little as an hour or two, to give a second opinion on customers' investment mix, for example, or to analyze whether they're saving enough for retirement.

Fee-only advisors are also distinguished by their tendency to provide holistic guidance. They care about clients' investments, but also about factors such as their debt and their income. A broker, on the other hand, is more likely to focus on customers' investments and insurance because those products generate commissions.

One of the few drawbacks of working with a fee-only financial planner is that they often aren't licensed to sell you investments or buy them on your behalf. They can provide you with an investment plan, but you may have to buy and, when appropriate, sell the stocks, bonds, and other investments yourself. Further consideration should be given to the size of a fee-only planner's operation, as many operate sole-proprietorships or very small businesses.

Other Options

Regional brokerages. Regional firms, with names like Raymond James, Ameriprise Financial, and Janney

Montgomery Scott, are simply smaller versions of Wall Street brokerage firms. Their business models are often as conflicted as those of their larger brethren, and they may have fewer resources to offer clients.

Independent broker-dealers. As their name implies, IBDs are brokers who don't work for national or regional firms. Instead, they work as independent contractors, affiliating with larger companies for things like trade execution and technology support. But they run their businesses under their own names and position themselves as a more trustworthy alternative to wirehouses or regional brokerages. IBDs may not face pressure to push particular products, but most still operate under a fundamental conflict: They earn commissions for selling products, and some products pay more than others.

Hybrid (or dually registered) advisors. Hybrid advisors can offer commission-based service as well as fee-based service; they are registered with both FINRA and the SEC. Advisors typically choose the hybrid model so that they can cater to clients who prefer either payment model. Hybrid advisors use the product platforms of RIAs for the fee-side of their business and of a broker-dealer for the commission side of their business. Because of this, hybrids can boast that they can offer more products and services than other advisors. However, doing so raises the specter of what is commonly referred to as "hat switching." How does one know whether the hybrid advisor is acting as a legal fiduciary—putting the client's interests first—or as a broker, finding a "suitable" product that may meet the client's needs but pays more to the advisor? The law allows them to be both with the same client and in the same meeting. Unfortunately, they don't really wear hats or switch them, so your guess is as good as mine.

Technology's Triumph

Not long ago, there was only one way to access the investment markets: Hire a broker and pay him fat commissions to buy and sell stocks. Through the mid-1970s, cheap, do-it-yourself investing was inconceivable. Then came "May Day."

On May 1, 1975, a decree from the Securities and Exchange Commission cracked open the brokerage market. The SEC's decision deregulated the industry, abolishing high-fixed fees for stock trades and paving the way for robust market competition. May Day eventually gave rise to the online discount brokerage business—and to vigorous competition on trading fees among the likes of Charles Schwab, E*Trade, Scottrade, and Ameritrade. Vying to attract business, industry players steadily lowered their rates: Schwab charged $60 per trade in 1998, for example, but by 2012, each of the major players charged less than $10 per trade.

The democratization of investing took another huge leap forward with the advent of the online brokerage in 1994. Today, investors can cheaply, and almost instantly, buy and sell stocks, bonds, mutual funds, and options online or on their mobile device. They can easily identify the management costs of their investments, pinpoint investments' performance history, and consult research reports, all of which enables them to make smarter choices. They can even use "back-testing" tools to find out if their investment strategies have been successful in various market conditions in the past.

The Wall Street stockbroker is no longer the gatekeeper who charges a stiff toll for access to the markets. Thanks to discount online brokerage, the markets are more accessible and transparent than ever. And individual investors have been empowered like never before.

Over the past few years, things have gotten even more exciting. We are now seeing the advent of online, software-based investment services that manage virtually the entire investing process. These services are far less expensive than a flesh-and-blood advisor and much simpler than managing your own stocks and bonds. And unlike many flesh-and-blood advisors, applications like Betterment, FutureAdvisor, PersonalCapital, MarketRiders, and Wealthfront have absolutely no conflict of interest. (I'll discuss these software-based investment services in more detail in Chapter 7.)

My fellow wealth advisors probably won't appreciate my saying this, but a certain percentage of investors would be better off handling their own investing. It's very possible to achieve competitive investment returns on your own, provided that you do two things: First, take the time to understand how to approach investing, and second, remain disciplined as you invest. Are those simple rules? Absolutely— and yet most people simply cannot follow them. As I'll explain shortly, most of us lack the ability to overcome the psychological and emotional wiring that leads to bad investing decisions. And that's true whether we're doing the investing ourselves or relying on software to do it.

The fact is, however, that the majority of investors are better off with the services of a qualified advisor. Why are advisors worth the money you'll pay them? Well, most aren't, frankly. But the best ones have abilities that you probably don't. The first is investment discipline or the ability to resist—and help you resist—the knee-jerk emotional decisions that invariably lead to bad results.

Second, they can save you a bundle of money in both the short term and the long term through shrewd tax management. And finally, a qualified advisor can show you ways to shield your estate against taxes and pass the maximum amount of your assets to your heirs or charity or any combination of the two.

Having read this far in this book, of course, you may be disinclined to trust any advisor. The conflicts of interest and hidden agendas among brokerages, banks, and asset managers are excellent reasons to be wary. And while there is much to be said for fee-based advisors, they're not the answer, either, because almost half of them are sole proprietors, or the majority have very small teams. Many simply lack the resources to properly serve a client's needs.

But if there weren't any trustworthy advisors in the industry, I wouldn't have bothered writing this book. In fact, I'd probably have left the industry altogether, years ago. Experience has taught me that there are trustworthy advisors, like diamonds in the rough, throughout the country and in each discipline. They might not get a lot of headlines—but in the age of Bernie Madoff, Allen Stanford, and countless other well-known rogues—that's probably a good thing.

The best advisors possess a combination of skills, experience, and commitment to their clients. They're a different breed from the majority of advisors, who are in the business mainly to enrich themselves. In a better world, these exceptional advisors would be the norm.

So, without just relying on pure luck, how do consumers find these advisors? The first step is simple—it's all about the business model. The Wall Street business model that I've described has conflicts of interest at its center, and you should generally avoid it. But there's a competing business model. It is designed *specifically to eliminate conflicts of interest*. It's increasingly being embraced by advisors who want to do what's right for their clients. And that brings us back to the Registered Investment Advisors (RIAs)—specifically, independent RIAs.

Key Points

There are many flavors of financial advisors that consumers can choose from. Each has its own pros and cons. Areas to pay special attention to include:

- Banks
  - Conflicts of interest—using their own products and asset management solutions.
  - Banks often pay their advisors less than they can earn elsewhere, which explains the low quality of many bank advisors.
- Trust companies and bank trust companies
  - Watch out for the "fox guarding the hen-house." Trust companies may try to use in-house investment products/solutions, which is a major conflict of interest.
- Asset managers
  - Asset managers who act as your advisor will never fire themselves regardless of performance. That's an inherent conflict of interest.
  - Better alternatives to asset managers can include simple, tax-efficient index mutual funds and exchange-traded funds.

- Insurance salesmen
  - Some may offer investment advice, but that's typically not their core business. Even if they are skilled at wealth advisory, the compensation for selling insurance is significantly higher, creating a conflict of interest.
  - Their primary compensation is selling insurance. Guess what is often the best solution for any need . . . ?
- Fee-only planners
  - Good news—no conflicts of interest!
  - Pay close attention to the size and depth of their organization.
- Wirehouse brokers, independent brokers, regional brokers
  - Often commission-based, which could pose a conflict of interest.
  - Often employ a limited set of choices (despite how they may spin this fact).

Chapter 5

The Case for Independent RIAs

What if there was an alternative reality in which car salesmen were paragons of trust? When you entered a dealership, you'd know that you would soon drive off the lot with the absolute best car for you. You'd have a car that's right for your budget, your family size, and your driving needs—at an unquestionably fair price.

Your "transportation advisor" might even suggest another manufacturer as opposed to his company. Sounds nice, right?

In reality, of course, nearly everyone who's ever bought a car from a dealer has driven off the lot feeling slightly queasy. We know that we've likely left money on the table—the only question is how much? Is there anyone who really, fully trusts car dealers to deliver the absolute best solution at the best price?

Most of us understand that, as helpful and friendly as our car dealers may appear, their agenda is clear: Their objective is to sell cars (plus add-ons like undercoating and extended warranties) at a price that will fetch the highest commission. We all know that the car dealer–to customer relationship is not a partnership. It's much more like a contest.

If only consumers were as guarded and cynical about financial advisors. As you understand very well by now, the world of financial advisors includes many, many people who are more interested in their own success than in their customers' success. Yet most Americans are under the illusion that their stock-brokers and even insurance salespeople are "fiducia-ries." In other words, most of us mistakenly believe that the people we buy investments and insurance from often put our interests ahead of their own.

This startling fact was made clear in a national study in 2010 by Infogroup/ORC. The results showed that:

- Two out of three U.S. investors believe, incorrectly, that stockbrokers are held to a fiduciary standard of client care.
- Three out of five mistakenly think that "insurance agents" have a fiduciary duty to their clients.
- Three-quarters of respondents believe that "financial advisors" must adhere to a fiduciary standard.

No wonder it's become standard practice for brokers to refer to themselves as financial advisors—it's a simple shortcut to engendering trust.

Most of the brokers, insurance agents, and others that the public believes are fiduciaries have no legal obligation to act as a fiduciary and most don't even come close to meeting the definition of a fiduciary. As articulated by the Institute for The Fiduciary Standard, a Virginia-based think tank, a fiduciary has six key duties:

1. Serve the client's best interest.
2. Act in utmost good faith.
3. Act prudently—with the care, skill, and judgment of a professional.

4. Avoid conflicts of interest.
5. Disclose all material facts.
6. Control investment expenses.

Only two groups within the financial advice industry truly have the ability to meet that definition of a fiduciary. One group is fee-only planners, whom you met in Chapter 4. Fee-only planners' pay-by-the-hour compensation arrangements typically remove all potential for conflicts of interest. By and large, these folks are in the business for all the right reasons.

The Trouble with Fee-Only Advisors

Yet fee-only advisors are not a panacea for investors. For starters, as mentioned previously, most fee-only advisor firms are tiny. As of 2009, half the membership of the fee-only advisor industry group, NAPFA, consisted of one-person practices. Another 25 percent consisted of practices with between four and six professionals; those firms managed or influenced an average of $105 million of client assets—meaning the firms were, by industry standards, pretty small.

Size shouldn't matter in choosing an advisor, but it does. Unfortunately, resources matter and small firms are likely to be resource-constrained. A large financial advisor practice has the key resources of money and (usually) broad expertise. These firms can afford the kinds of research and technology that allow them to give better advice, make better decisions, and provide better service on your behalf. What's more, a team of advisors, as opposed to a one- or two-person firm, is more likely to include experts in areas beyond just investing. A bigger firm might house experts in tax management, trust, estate planning, and other important areas. And some firms have staff that do nothing but perform investment research.

Most smaller firms are not able to provide the same level of sophisticated advice and service that larger ones can; after all, it's all but impossible for one individual to truly be an expert in investment management, tax, trust, and estate planning. And that constraint makes it more difficult on a practical level for small firms to fulfill the fiduciary obligation of serving their clients' best interests.

Furthermore, many fee-only advisors do not offer investment management services, meaning their clients must invest their own money or find a third party to do it for them. Not offering investing services is certainly not a breach of fiduciary duty—in fact, many fee-only advisors don't offer investment management

precisely because they don't want even the appearance of a possible conflict of interest. But it's simply
inconvenient for clients to get their advice in one
place and have their investments managed elsewhere.
That's a big reason why, in my experience, very few
wealthy investors use fee-only advisors.

Another fundamental drawback of small firms has
to do with continuity. One-man shops, in particular,
should be a red flag for clients who want long-term
relationships. Many sole practitioners cannot put
succession plans in place. Often these advisors became
sole practioners or small business operators for a
reason. They like their solitary arrangement and don't
want to spend their time grooming a successor. And,
the truth is that it's typically difficult for them to find a
suitable candidate, because small, poorly resourced
firms are not attractive to young, ambitious advisors.
So no matter how successful the relationship with
your fee-only advisor is, the fact is that you may well
be forced to start shopping for a new advisor on the
day he or she is no longer available.

The Case for Independent RIAs

The group whose business model is most closely
aligned with the fiduciary standard is one that, from

the outside, might seem similar to brokers. Like brokers, independent RIAs provide advice and manage your investments. RIAs and brokers might dress the same; they might chat you up about golf in the same way; their offices might be indistinguishable. But RIAs and brokers are very, very different. The key distinction is an invisible but critical one, and it has to do with the fact that RIAs and brokers answer to two very different regulators.

The RIA model has its roots in the 1929 stock market crash. In the wake of that calamity, Congress convened hearings into its causes; the resulting testimony brought to light widespread insider trading, stock price manipulation, and other abusive practices that served to separate investors from their money.

To help protect the investing public from these abuses, Congress in 1934 created the Securities and Exchange Commission. The SEC is responsible for policing the securities business, and among those it regulates are RIAs. That's a good thing for investors to know: Firms that choose to register with the SEC must adhere to the 1940 Act and its associated fiduciary standard of care—they must act in clients' best interests and must disclose, if not eliminate, any conflicts of interest.

As you know, brokers are held to a much looser standard of client care—the "suitability standard." Their regulator, FINRA, is what's known as a "self-regulatory organization." In other words, it's the brokerage industry policing itself—or as I suggested earlier, the prisoners running the prison (or the patients running the asylum, take your pick). It's not surprising that FINRA has so vigorously fought attempts to bring its members under the more stringent fiduciary standard—the standard would completely undercut its business model, a model that is highly profitable, often at the expense of the consumer.

It's important to understand that those who are regulated by the SEC have actively made that choice. An RIA, by definition, is a person or firm that is registered with, and thus held to the fiduciary standard by, the SEC.[1] It's simple, and often more profitable, to become a broker by passing some tests and then joining a brokerage firm or setting up an independent practice. But RIAs have consciously chosen

---

[1]RIAs with over $100 million under management/advisement must register with the SEC, while smaller firms are state-regulated.

to work under a model that is known to be less conflicted than the brokerage model. And, as you learned in Chapter 3, the number of RIAs has increased by 31 percent, to nearly 21,000 since 2004. A great number of those new RIAs are reformed brokers won over by the industry's culture of "clients before profits."

And RIAs are well aware that their fiduciary status can help them win new business. In a 2011 survey by TD Ameritrade Holdings, RIAs cited their fiduciary status as the biggest single reason new clients join them. For their part, consumers seem to be becoming more and more aware of the standard. Twenty-nine percent of advisors who were queried in the 2011 study said the fiduciary standard was the top reason they won new clients. That was up from 15 percent just half a year earlier.

Other top reasons RIAs gave for attracting new clients were the competitive fee structure offered at an RIA firm (21 percent) and dissatisfaction with full-commission brokers (19 percent).

Being a fiduciary means more than just having the intent to put clients' interests first. Advisors registered with the SEC or its state counterparts must work within businesses that are set up in concrete ways to adhere to the 1940 Act fiduciary standard. RIAs' compensation system is a prime example. RIA advisors typically provide investment advice for a fee—they are not paid, as brokers are, for selling or buying securities for clients. In industry parlance, the arrangement puts advisors and clients "on the same side of the table" as the consumer.

RIAs also differ from brokers and asset managers with respect to where clients' cash and investments are housed. By using a third-party custodian, typical RIAs don't have access to the cash or securities that clients entrust to them. Properly structured, an advisor can buy and sell investments on your behalf, but cannot get hold of your funds. That's because a third party, the aforementioned custodian, typically holds RIAs' clients' assets. Some of the bigger custodians used by RIAs include Fidelity, Schwab, and TD Ameritrade (you may know these firms best for their operations other than custody—mutual funds and discount brokerage).

Bernard Madoff was able to run his Ponzi scheme because he held clients' cash in his own brokerage firm. Madoff would simply dip into new clients' money to pay supposed investment profits to older clients. And since Madoff controlled the statements his clients received, he simply fabricated monies that did not exist. Having another party act as a custodian inserts an additional *check and balance* to protect the consumer, and at no additional expense to the investor.

This is not to say that the major wirehouses such as Merrill Lynch, Morgan Stanley, Smith Barney, Goldman Sachs, LPL Financial, and other major players are risky places to house your assets; rather, smaller brokerage operations, where custody and control reside with one group, invite additional risk.

Such safeguards help to ensure that advisors stay on the right side of the ethical line. And of course, advisors who work against clients' best interests are subject to punishment from the SEC, which has the ability to recommend criminal investigations.

Buyer Beware

Should you be impressed by an advisor's RIA title? Not necessarily. True, the title means he or she isn't a broker, and for that reason, it may be worth your time to learn more about them. But the truth is that earning the title is surprisingly easy—in fact, it's far too easy.

For perspective, consider what's required to become a practicing physician. Aspiring physicians are typically required to undergo four years at a university, four years of medical school, and three to seven years of internship and residency. Upon receiving their MDs, they must swear to the Hippocratic Oath, promising to uphold their profession honestly and ethically. Practicing physicians then face between 10 and 50 hours per year of required continuing medical education.

Contrast that with becoming a practicing RIA. To enter the industry, about 20 years ago, I had to pass a test that the average person could study for in a few hours. The test did not contribute significantly to my ability to serve my clients; studying for it taught me very little. And neither I nor any of my RIA counterparts across the country are required to undergo any continuing education that is not self-administered. The standards for becoming and remaining an RIA haven't changed a bit in decades.

Should it really be the case that your doctor, dentist, accountant, and lawyer face rigorous preparation and ongoing education while the person entrusted with protecting your financial future can do so after just a few hours' preparation? Of course not. The bar to becoming an RIA (or a broker, for that matter) is so low that it's an embarrassment to the profession. I am, of course, speaking of the minimum threshold to become a financial advisor. There are certainly good advisors that continually work to sharpen their skills and serve their clients as best they can. The problem is that investing consumers have no idea how to differentiate a good salesperson from a well-qualified advisor.

And, for what it's worth, even when advisors earn continuing education designations, it's hard for consumers to judge how significant these designations are. Advisors are proud to festoon their business cards with credentials like CIMA, CFP, CFA, CPWA, ChFC, and CLU, among many other industry designations. These are legitimate certifications—and I applaud the advisors who earn them. But the fact is that most consumers can learn little from the alphabet soup that follows advisor names—these designations don't reflect what advisors have learned or how many hours of study they've invested. Evaluating advisors' skill levels is a major challenge, if not an impossibility, for consumers.

Matt Corrado © 2013

Alphabet Soup . . . what does it all mean?

Do All RIAs Live Up to Their Title?

The RIA portion of the investment industry isn't wholly composed of saints. Advisors who are hungry for more profit than the current business model allows can use an enormous legal loophole to get what they want—all while staying on the right side of the law. The loophole is as simple as it is absurd: RIAs cannot have conflicts of interest—*unless they disclose those conflicts*. And, amazingly, as long as the conflicts are disclosed, *the RIAs are still considered to have complied with the 1940 Act and the fiduciary standard.*

In other words, an advisor can look clients in the eye and assure them that he's a fiduciary, bound to put their interest ahead of his own, even though he operates under clear conflicts of interest. The fiduciary loophole means that egregious conflicts of interest are fine and dandy, just as long as they are disclosed.

And, to make matters worse, studies by Yale University's Daylian Cain and others show that disclosing conflicts of interest can have the perverse effect of *engendering confidence*. Simply illustrated, a disclosure by an advisor admitting that he profits more by recommending lesser product B versus product A will likely yield a response such as, "Wow, my financial advisor sure is honest, because he told me that he gets paid three times as much by using product B instead of product A." It's a simple fact, backed up by Cain's research, that this "sales maneuver" actually inspires misplaced confidence.

Now, if you think the "avoid or disclose" approach means your advisor must tell you about his conflicts of interest face to face, you're sadly mistaken. These kinds of awkward conversations almost never take place. Instead, the disclosures are tucked into documents that are known for their mind-numbing legalese. It's safe to say that few investors read these documents and those that do rarely understand just what they're reading.

If investors actually read and understood RIAs' disclosure documents, they'd find that a shocking number of supposed fiduciaries can legally receive:

- **Brokerage commissions.** Incredible but true. RIAs just need to affiliate with a brokerage company and make the proper disclosures (in legalese, naturally), and they're free to sell you investments that pay them sales commissions.

- **"Soft-dollar" compensation** from firms they do business with. Advisors partner with third parties to provide all kinds of investment and research services. As fiduciaries, they should choose service providers based purely on which provide the best service at the lowest cost. These third parties can't legally "pay to play" by offering advisors cash to do business with them. But they can offer "free" research or pay for the Bloomberg machine and other services in what's known as *soft-dollar* compensation.

- **Payments from third parties** that can only be described as "kickbacks." Advisors partner with companies that make sure the mechanics of buying and selling investments happen properly. Fees for these services are charged to customers' accounts—*that's you*. So advisors should partner with the best and lowest-cost providers. But providers and advisors can participate in sweetheart deals in which providers return a portion of the fees clients pay to the advisor. It's a stealth way of advisors picking your pocket to further enrich themselves.

Disorienting Disclosure

Just for fun, let's take a look at the 2012 disclosure document from a large and successful advisor firm in California that describes itself—quite legally—as a fiduciary. The firm's "ADV, Part 2" form (through which the SEC mandates that RIAs must describe their firm in plain English), describes a smorgasbord of conflicts of interest. Following are a few choice excerpts from the form—along with my translations of the supposed plain English into *actual* plain English. (I've replaced references to the firm's name with a pseudonym.)

> Clients will be charged brokerage commissions (for equity transactions), ticket charges

(which are applied to most transactions), and, for mutual funds, ETFs or other pooled investment vehicles will incur the fund expenses incurred by the fund. Advisor's fees are exclusive of brokerage commissions, transaction fees, and other related costs and expenses which will be incurred by the client. For trades in equity securities where Advisor has the authority to determine or select the broker, clients pay the same commission rate, whether the transaction is executed through

We believe in transparency, just read these . . .

ACME AMERICAN SECURITIES LLC (Advisor's affiliated broker-dealer [AAS]) or through a prime or executing broker. Because the commission rate established by AAS is negotiated between Advisor and AAS, there are inherent limitations in that negotiation process.

In plain English: *We charge you a fee to provide advice and then we charge you again (and again) when you act on that advice.*

Due to the common ownership between Advisor and AAS, when AAS receives a fee or commission the economic benefit will be received by the owners of Advisor. This presents a conflict of interest in that it may create an incentive to recommend investment products or funds based on the compensation received rather than solely on the needs of the client. . . . Advisor does not reduce its advisory fee to offset any Rule 12b-1 fee, commissions, or other expense incurred by clients except as required by applicable law.

In plain English: *We get paid extra when we sell you certain things. Don't say we didn't tell you that we choose those investments because we get paid more. Oh, and when we do earn more, we keep 100 percent of that extra revenue for ourselves.*

> Advisor may have a motivation to refer clients to invest in a fund for which AAM receives a performance or management fee.

In plain English: *Sometimes we'll cut deals with other asset management firms. When we do, rest assured that their investments will probably be in your portfolio. That way we make more money.*

> (Advisor's) advisory affiliate, AAM, receives performance fees, either directly or indirectly, from the funds for which it acts as general partner or otherwise participates in the ownership of the general partner of the fund. . . . Performance-based fee arrangements may create an incentive for Advisor or AAM to recommend investments which may be riskier or more speculative than those which would be recommended under a different fee

arrangement. Such fee arrangements also create an incentive to favor higher fee paying accounts over other accounts in the allocation of investment opportunities. All clients will be treated fairly and, to the extent feasible, uniformly (subject to the investment objectives, restrictions, and risk tolerance of the different clients).

In plain English: *Did I mention that some of the stuff we will recommend (or just place in your account if you give us discretion) pays us for using them? In fact, if they actually perform, we get paid even more.*

On a very limited basis, and only with disclosure and client consent, Advisor will receive compensation for recommending another adviser to client.

In plain English: *If we send you to a lawyer, CPA, or other professional, they may pay us a referral fee. Chances are that will drive our choice more than who the best resource is for you. We'll probably put the disclosure page in the stack with all of the other ones. P.S. Don't forget that you're supposed to read all of this stuff.*

For those clients who elect to custody cash and securities elsewhere, ABC Corp. may, at the direction of Advisor, assist in clearing trades to settle at client's designated custodial broker or bank. ABC Corp. imposes ticket charges on trades that are cleared through ABC Corp. and these charges are paid by clients, which fee is remitted to ABC Corp. AAS receives a portion of the interest charged on debit balances and short positions by ABC Corp., certain additional credits, a portion of the interest paid on client accounts, and a portion of the rebates paid to ABC Corp. by money market funds in which cash in client accounts may be invested, unless prohibited by applicable law.

Clients of Advisor generally will authorize and direct it to execute securities transactions through AAS as introducing broker. AAS will receive commissions for client trades that it handles as well as income and other benefits resulting from AAS's clearing agreement with ABC Corp. AAS will also receive fees for acting as placement agent for pooled investment vehicles in which clients of Advisor invest. By virtue of the common ownership of Advisor and AAS, the executive officers and owners of Advisor will indirectly receive (through the corresponding ownership of AAS) the economic benefit of the commissions and other sources of income noted above. In addition, AAS may choose to pay a portion of these commissions and this income to its registered representatives, who are also employed by Advisor. As a result of the common ownership and payment of commissions, AAS may have a conflict of interest in limiting commissions and other transaction costs when executing brokerage transactions for advisory clients. Moreover, due to the common ownership between Advisor and AAS, there are inherent limitations regarding the negotiation of commission rates for transactions handled by AAS.

In plain English: *You will use our custodian. And, instead of getting you a better price, we keep some of your interest expense, transaction costs, and whatever else we can get our hands on.*

Soft Dollar Practices

Consistent with obtaining best execution for clients, Advisor may direct brokerage transactions for clients' portfolios to brokers who provide research and execution services to Advisor and, indirectly, to Advisor's clients. These services generally would be of the type described in Section 28(e) of the Securities Exchange Act of 1934 and are designed to augment Advisor's own internal research and investment strategy capabilities. Advisor does not generally attempt to put a specific dollar value on the services rendered or to allocate the relative costs or benefits of those services among clients, believing that the research it receives will help Advisor to fulfill its overall duty to its clients.

In plain English: *We pick some of the people we do business with based on what they are willing to give us. Some buy us research, some buy us computers or subscriptions, and sometimes we figure out other ways they can pay for stuff. We know we should probably give those savings to you, but heck . . . we like to make money.*

In particular, to the extent that orders are placed with broker/dealers from which Advisor receives a benefit (including AAS), the commission rates, clearing and execution costs for client account transactions, and correspondingly the rates and costs clients pay, may not be as favorable as the rates and execution costs that Advisor might be able to obtain at broker/dealers that do not provide Advisor with such benefits."

"AAS earns transaction-based compensation and this compensation results in an economic benefit to Advisor. AAS acts as placement agent for the funds, including those for which AAM acts as general partner or other corporate affiliate. For that role AAS receives a fee from fund that would otherwise have been payable to AAM as management or performance fees. (Clients do not pay "twice" for such services). The ownership of AAS is the same as for Advisor. . . .

In plain English: *Tired of hearing how we make money off of your account over and above your fee and how it affects our decisions? Sorry, here are a few more ways.*

In a limited number of circumstances, Advisor may provide payment to a third-party for referring prospective clients to Advisor.

In plain English: *Your other advisors may be on the take, too.*

I'm not aware of any other industry whose members are allowed to act contrary to their stated mission. Policemen aren't allowed to run gambling operations in their spare time. Doctors aren't allowed to prolong your illness so they can keep billing you. But advisors can call themselves fiduciaries while working against your interests and picking your pocket and it's all nice and legal. That is why knowing that your advisor is an RIA, and that he or she is technically a fiduciary, is not enough. A better, clearer standard for evaluating advisors is sorely needed. Simple standards that make a black-and-white distinction between conflicted and unconflicted[2] advisors are long overdue.

---

[2]Technically, there is never a pure conflict-free relationship with an advisor. Simply negotiating your fee is a conflict. However, in the context of our discussion, unconflicted refers to advisors who are not motivated to make a recommendation of any sort based on their personal compensation.

RIAs: A Good Place to Start

"Democracy," Winston Churchill famously said, "is the worst form of government—with the exception of all the others." So it is with the financial advice industry. RIAs are not all perfect, and yes, there are a few bad apples in the bushel. The industry's standards for skill should be higher, and it's too easy for advisors to pose as fiduciaries when they're not.

But in choosing among the countless advisors vying to manage your money, you've got to start somewhere. And the RIA sphere is the best place to start. In an industry plagued by conflicts of interest, the RIA model's use of the fiduciary standard, a consumer-friendly fee structure and its culture of *clients before profits* set it apart. But an important job remains: separating the elite RIAs from the rest. How do we separate the charlatans from the truly capable?

Key Points

- Independent RIAs, regulated by the SEC, are a small but growing segment of the market. However, most investors don't even know this option exists.

- RIAs supervised by the SEC are held to the fiduciary standard; although there exists a giant loophole they can exploit.
- Many fee-only planners (who are also fiduciaries) operate very small businesses and may be resource-constrained.
- There is virtually no barrier to entry to becoming or remaining an RIA.
- The giant loophole—"avoid or disclose"—allows conflicted advisors to meet the fiduciary standard. Beware of RIAs that bury disclosures in their public disclosure documents (specifically their Form ADV, which they must offer you when you meet them). Fancy language and a mountain of paper hides many a conflict.

Chapter 6

Our Lazy Brains: Why We're So Bad at Choosing Advisors (and Investing Our Own Money)

Over the course of my career, I've learned plenty about how unscrupulous or unqualified advisors can damage their clients. But I've also learned that investors themselves are often their own worst enemies. Take one of my first clients, for example.

In my early days as an advisor, my biggest challenge was attracting customers. To get prospects in the door, I'd offer a "free investment performance analysis." Basically, I'd look at three years of transactions, analyzing performance and asset allocation (how the investments in the portfolio balanced risk and reward), and provide a second opinion on how well the prospects' investment advisor was managing their investments.

My hope, frankly, was to find that my competition was doing a lousy job—which would conveniently allow me to position myself as an alternative. When an advisor seemed to be serving his or her client well, of course, I told the client so. Unfortunately, in most cases, I found a lack of diversification and a bias toward products that were better for the broker than the client. As a result, my new business was booming.

One day, a fellow I'll call "Joe" was introduced to me and took me up on my offer. Like many wealthy people, Joe had his money invested with more than one advisor. His instructions to me were simple: Evaluate which of his two advisors was doing a better job managing his wealth. He planned to fire one and keep the other.

It turned out to be an easy assignment. One of the two investment advisors clearly loved to chase hot stocks: The mix of investments that he bought and sold in Joe's account had risen and fallen steeply over the years, a risky approach that had yielded a net result of mediocre long-term performance.

The other advisor? He had done virtually everything right. He'd put Joe's money in an appropriate mix of stocks and bonds. He hadn't traded excessively, which meant he'd avoided racking up brokerage fees and undermining long-term performance. Over the years, advisor #2 had delivered performance that was clearly superior to that of advisor #1.

I sat down with Joe to explain the results without having yet had the opportunity to identify which manager was which. "This is great," he said. "Now I'll finally have the ammunition to fire the manager I don't like and move my money to the one I do like." I reported to Joe that it was no contest; he should consolidate his assets with advisor #2. Joe was taken aback. He'd been certain that the manager he didn't connect with on a personal level was the one to fire. The successful money manager, he explained, just wasn't charismatic enough. Joe had it exactly backward.

I thought, "Who cares about his personality? You spend *results*, not personality." I wonder whether Joe would reject a successful brain surgeon on the basis of being a dull dinner companion?

For me, the *Joe* episode has come to symbolize the fact that, when it comes to money, humans can be hopelessly irrational and extremely emotional. Most often, it's the best salesperson—not the best advisor—who wins the business. Based purely on the numbers and on the facts, Joe's choice of advisors was an easy call. But he wanted a different outcome. And, had I not been there to underscore what was important, he likely would have fired the wrong manager. This is but one example of emotion driving an outcome that should be based on math and on facts. Unfortunately, there are lots of Joes out there. There's a good chance you may be one of them.

Consumers make irrational and shortsighted choices about their money every day, and that includes the way we choose advisors. The vast majority of consumers who select advisors do so based on superficial, emotional factors rather than the solid factual criteria that really matter. Likewise, humans regularly make irrational, shortsighted investing decisions when managing investments themselves. The result is that we undermine our chances of achieving our long-term financial goals, and in the worst-case scenario, we risk losing our money outright.

Why is this, you might ask? Aren't Homo sapiens supposed to be the smart species? The answer is yes . . . except when we're not.

The Gut versus the Mind

The brain is the most powerful computer on Earth. Think about it. Your brain continuously processes information that is pouring in simultaneously through all five senses. At the same time, it coordinates respiration, circulation, balance and movement, digestion, the production and distribution of hormones and other chemicals. Your brain directs your body to fend off germs and to heal itself. It allows you to communicate and experience emotions. It lets you think, analyze, and solve problems. And, when operating at its full capacity, your brain makes you self-aware.

The brain is awesome. But when it comes to choosing advisors, our brain usually does a decidedly half-assed job, and our emotion—that "gut check" that is referenced so often—takes over. When we're choosing someone to entrust our financial health we desperately need our brain's capacity for logic and critical thinking. But, like friends who vanish just as a bar fight is brewing, these faculties seem to desert us when we need them most.

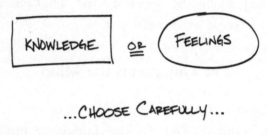

In fact, when it comes to serious thinking, our brains are just plain lazy. In his book *Thinking Fast and Slow*, Daniel Kahneman explains that while the mind has an exceptional capacity for logic and critical thinking, it uses that power sparingly. The mind, Kahneman explains, is always looking for shortcuts, always trying to avoid the heavy lifting that active thinking requires. To paraphrase Winston Churchill, the mind will only resort to serious thinking once it has exhausted the alternatives.

To explain how the mind works, Kahneman uses the analogy that it contains two systems that drive the way we think. These systems reason about the world in different ways and are meant to complement each other. System 1's reasoning is automatic, intuitive, emotional, and fast; it tells us that one dog walking our way is friendly but another is to be avoided. It lets us finish a phrase like "bread and . . . ____ " instantly and effortlessly. System 2, on the other hand, is slow, conscious, and analytical, and requires deliberate effort.

When you're filling out a tax return or taking a test, System 2 is in charge.

Which part of your mental machinery should be in charge when you're choosing an advisor? Clearly, it's System 2. But System 2 tires easily and often becomes overburdened—which is why it frequently defers to System 1, Kahneman explains:

> . . . when System 2 is otherwise engaged, we will believe almost anything. System 1 is gullible and biased to believe, System 2 is in charge of doubting and unbelieving, but System 2 is sometimes busy, and often lazy. (*Thinking, Fast and Slow*, p. 81)

The way the two systems work makes sense from an evolutionary perspective: Higher thinking takes so much energy and effort that it's far more efficient and requires less energy to let System 1 sort through most of the information we're bombarded with daily.

The fact that the analytical mind often doesn't kick in when it should is a boon for salesmen. This "lazy" tendency in prospects' mental machinery allows advisors to win customers through salesmanship alone. Before hiring an advisor, every consumer should pepper the candidates with tough questions— everything from how they're paid to how they manage portfolio risk to what their succession plan is. If advisor candidates give vague answers, potential clients should demand clarification. In interviewing a potential advisor, System 2 should be fully in charge.

But System 2 often isn't running the show. For whatever reason—maybe because they feel overmatched by what they assume is the advisor's superior knowledge and expertise or because *they don't know what they don't know*—potential clients typically are not in the careful, analytical frame of mind they should be as they meet with potential new advisors.

That leaves them vulnerable to salesmanship. Most successful advisors are skilled in the art of persuading people to give them their business. Think about it: We typically do business with people we *like*, as opposed to choosing those who are best at what they do. That's what Joe planned to do. If you have an advisor or broker, think back to how you chose him or her.

Salesmanship 101

Effective salespeople know that a simple way to win over a potential client is to get him saying yes—or at least get the client nodding his head. I recall learning that if you can get a prospect to say "yes" seven times, then your likelihood of completing a sale goes up exponentially. Achieving that is simple: Just ask questions or make statements to which the only possible response is "yes" or "I agree." A nod of the head counts as a success.

Here's an idea of how such conversations typically go when advisors are doing the selling.

Advisor: I've been dealing with wealthy clients for many years. Most of these folks share some common goals. Rule #1 is that they want to be able to maintain their lifestyle *no matter what*.

Potential client: (Nods head, thinking, *Yep, that's me.*)

Advisor: They want to minimize taxes. . . .

Potential client: (Nodding head) Yep.

Yep, that's us. You got it. Uh-huh. Exactly!

Advisor: And they want to protect their wealth so they can pass it on to their kids and/or charity, but not the government.

Potential client: (Nodding head) Exactly.

For those of you keeping score, that's three head nods in response to three statements. All the statements are aimed at the potential client's emotions, certainly not at their intellect. (Is there any wealthy person who wants a less comfortable retirement, who wants to pay more taxes, who wants to leave everything to Uncle Sam? Well, there may be a few who want to disinherit their kids, but not very many.)

The questions are emotionally manipulative—and extremely effective. The potential client feels the advisor really "gets" him, and thanks to all that head-nodding, he's now in an agreeable frame of mind. After a few short platitudes about investment performance and client friendliness, the advisor typically has himself or herself a new client. Skeptical System 2, if it engages at all, does so too late to protect the consumer from potential harm.

Financial firms and their advertising teams know that it's often more effective to appeal to our intuitive, emotional, superficial thought processes than to our analytical ones. Remember Goldman Sachs's ad about renewable energy, with its tagline "Progress Is Everyone's Business"? It was aimed squarely at System 1.

By the way; big, powerful advisor firms *really* know how to get their customers to avoid critical thinking. Very big clients of firms like JPMorgan Chase find themselves gaining access to lunches with the likes of Bill Clinton and Tony Blair. With power perks like these, would many people be able to think critically about how well their advisor is doing his or her actual job and whether they're being charged fairly for the services they're receiving? Does System 2 even kick in to remind them that they are footing the bill—one way or another—for their cushy lunch and guest speaker?

What You See Is All There Is

Most consumers who sign on with a financial advisor do so without having all the facts they need. In fact, the real reason that the fast and superficial part of their brain takes over is because consumers simply don't know what to ask. How do you interview a lawyer? A doctor? Your financial advisor? These are all really important decisions, and most of us don't know the first thing to ask in order to narrow the field.

It's simply easier to follow our intuition. And as Kahneman explains, intuition doesn't need or want to consider too much information. It's lazy, and thus, so are we.

My personal experience with clients has taught me that *we often don't know what we don't know*. Clients don't know they should ask about their advisor's fee structure and where they truly add value, conflicts of interest, or succession plans, let alone ask about their compliance protocols or their training. They certainly don't know enough to test an advisor's knowledge of tax or estate planning. It's almost as though consumers interview potential advisors so that they can be told what to do and what to think.

Brokers certainly don't give prospective clients a *heads-up* that there's another business model out there with a higher standard of client care, that they might be conflicted by varied compensation, or that they aren't fully staffed to meet the client's needs.

And oftentimes, it's clear that clients, on an unconscious level, don't want to know. Why mess up that great story they're telling themselves—"I'm giving this advisor my business because he really understands me, we connect, and I trust him"—with information that might undermine that story and make their decision more complicated? Kahneman sees this phenomenon as so pervasive that he's dubbed it WYSIATI: What You See Is All There Is.

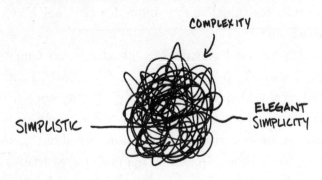

All successful salesmen, including advisors, understand WYSIATI on a gut level. They know intuitive mental machinery is wired to form conclusions without seeking complete evidence. That allows them to capitalize on it to win clients purely by offering them neat, persuasive stories—otherwise known as a sales pitch.

My Advisor Is Handsome, So Why Am I Broke?

In his 2005 bestselling book, *Blink: The Power of Thinking Without Thinking*, Malcolm Gladwell provides a vivid example of how using mental shortcuts to make an important decision can prove disastrous.

As you may know, Warren Harding is on every short list of the worst presidents in history. So how it is that Americans came to elect him in the first place? When Harding entered the race for the White House in 1920, he'd had an undistinguished political career. He wasn't known for his intelligence. He was a notorious womanizer. Gladwell explains the phenomenon that brought this mediocre playboy to power as "the Warren Harding error."

In short, Harding was extremely distinguished-looking and handsome, seemingly sprung to life off of a Roman coin. Based on that information, voters intuited that the man must be courageous, intelligent, and brimming with integrity. "They didn't dig below the surface," Gladwell writes. "The way he looked carried so many powerful connotations that it stopped the normal process of thinking dead in its tracks."

The Harding error is repeated over and over again in the financial advice industry. As consumers select advisors, they use mental shortcuts; they fail, as Gladwell puts it, to dig below the surface. The Harding error, writes Gladwell, is "why picking the right candidate for a job is so difficult and why, on more occasions than we may care to admit, utter mediocrities sometimes end up in positions of enormous responsibility."

Feel-Good Brokerage

Have you ever stopped to admire the packaging that brokerage firms use?

Their logos, designed to seem solid and strong; the polished look of their websites and marketing materials; the slick aesthetic of their offices. It's all very confidence inspiring.

But as the saying goes, "never judge a book by its cover." It stands to reason that brokerage firms focus on exterior looks because the results that the typical broker delivers are so often below average. By definition, the firm's legion of brokers will deliver average results, all under the same brand.

I can't get into this subject without bringing up a guy named Louis Cheskin. You might not recognize Cheskin's name, but he was a marketing revolutionary and the genius behind advertising icons like the Marlboro Man and the Gerber Baby.

Cheskin brought the world the concept of *sensation transference*—the idea that the packaging of a product influences consumers' attitude toward the product itself. You can find examples of sensation transference in every aisle of your supermarket.

Cheskin singlehandedly made the margarine industry by dyeing sticks of white vegetable fat and water yellow, in order to make them look like butter. He helped turn what had once been a woman's cigarette into a symbol of masculinity by developing the Marlboro Man. And he created the Gerber Baby.

Malcolm Gladwell, in his 2005 bestseller *Blink*, explains Cheskin's insight perfectly. The marketing man, he says, "believed that most of us don't make a distinction—on an unconscious level—between the package and the product. The product and the package are the product combined."

Make no mistake: The major financial companies are all about the packaging. Their look is crafted as carefully as the Gerber Baby by the best, most expensive advertising firms. I can't really blame them. If my business's model was riddled with conflicts of interest— so much so that insisting on lower standards for consumers was my best shot at survival— then substituting great packaging for a lousy product is exactly what I'd do.

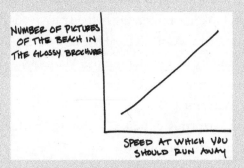

By the way, packaging goes far beyond marketing. Elements as minor as a uniform a professional person wears can carry a sub-conscious message: "I'm an authority in my field." And it's effective!

In his classic book on marketing research, *Influence: The Psychology of Persuasion*, Robert Cialdini describes a telling experiment on that subject. Researchers had a 31-year-old man cross a street in Texas against the traffic light on multiple occasions. Cialdini writes:

> In half of the cases, he was dressed in a freshly pressed business suit and tie; on the other occasions, he wore a work shirt and trousers. The researchers watched from a distance and counted the number of pedestrians waiting at the corner who followed the man across the street. Like the children of Hamelin who crowded after the Pied Piper, three and a half times as many people swept into traffic behind the suited jaywalker. In this case, though, the magic came not from his pipe but his pinstripes.

> The lesson? If your advisor wears a nice suit, it only means he dresses well, not that he's good at what he does.

Why We Stink at Managing Our Own Money

Most people just aren't very good at managing their own investments. They make investing decisions that are self-defeating, and they make the same mistakes over and over. Those decisions are based on the primal emotions of fear and greed, emotions so powerful and deep-rooted that they can destroy your investment plan and your self-discipline like a wave crashing into a sandcastle. You may recall that I've referred to these instincts as the emotions upon which the great marketers of products capitalize.

These emotions force us to abandon our patient, long-term plan. They prompt us to sell and buy stocks at exactly the wrong time. If this has happened to you, you've got a lot of company.

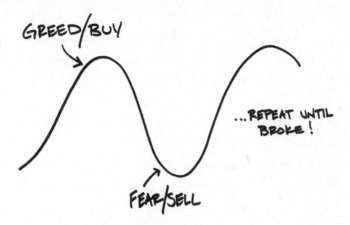

It's tempting to moralize about the self-defeating decisions that investors make. Investors who dump their stocks when the markets turn ominous? Clearly they lack self-discipline! Those who are so smitten by a single hot stock that they fail to diversify? They are greedy! Deep down, most of us are judgmental—especially of ourselves. We are even better at recognizing the things in others that we don't like about ourselves. Spot it in someone else and the chances are you suffer from the same condition (aka *spot it; you got it*)!

But moralizing and judgment are of zero help when it comes to investing. We can't shame ourselves into being better investors (and even if we could, our egos would rationalize our way out of it!). And the truth is that our self-defeating behavior isn't the result of moral weakness. It's simply the result of the way our brains are wired.

We humans like to talk about our "brain," in the singular. In fact, that gray mass in our skulls is better understood as three distinct regions (not to be confused with Kahneman's "two systems"). Each of the three brain regions represents a different stage in the evolution of our species. The primitive, so-called reptile region is responsible for our essential biological functions: breathing, heart activity, and temperature regulation. The most recently evolved region, the hominid brain, is the seat of rational thought, language, and mathematical ability. The hominid brain is where our rational, disciplined investing decisions are made. Unfortunately, it is often overruled by what's known as the mammalian brain. The mammalian brain is the seat of emotion. It's where we experience everything from love to hate to anger to surprise. As the brain's "fight-or-flight" region, it has played a key role in the survival of our species.

Clearly the mammalian brain is an asset, for lots of reasons. But when we humans turn to investing, it can be a huge handicap. As long as markets are stable or heading straight up as they do for short periods of time, it isn't hard for the average investor to remain disciplined, think long-term and stick to the plan. It's when conditions are volatile that we get into trouble.

In the course of a stressful event—whether it's an animal attack or a market sell-off—our ability to think clearly declines. In physiological terms, blood flow to the rational, hominid brain declines. Blood surges, meanwhile, to the primitive and mammalian regions of the brain. With the body in survival mode, the rational gives way to the irrational.

When confronted by a saber-tooth tiger, it is indeed probably better to run first and think later. When confronted by a crisis in the market, however, the impulse to action is usually not our friend. The short-term impulse to grab our nest egg and move it out of the path of oncoming trouble is all too understandable. But it's usually not the right decision: Too often, it results in selling at the absolutely wrong time. And that poorly timed selling is typically followed by an equally poorly timed return to the market. Locking in losses by selling when the market is tanking, and then buying back stocks at far higher prices, is a textbook example of the foibles of do-it-yourself investors.

Here's how that kind of panicked behavior can crush your investment portfolio. Say you have stock market investments of $1 million. The market has been sliding for two weeks, and so far it's off 15 percent—with no end in sight. With your portfolio down to $850,000, you give in to your instincts to pull your money out of the way of further harm.

You sell it all, and breathe a sigh of relief. Then, wouldn't you know it, the markets start to stabilize, and then, amazingly, begin to recover. You're not convinced the rally is real, so you keep what's left of your money on the sidelines. By the time you feel safe enough to get back in the game, you realize that buying back your investments will cost you $1 million. That loss of $150,000 on paper has become real. And you have your primal emotions to thank.

The truth is that as advanced as our mind's logical abilities are, emotions still rule the roost. They're the bully of the brain, pushing aside our best-laid plans in order to have their way. There are ways to avoid our inner emotional bullies, however. Earlier in this book, I described new online, software-based investment services that manage virtually the entire investing process. Part of the beauty of these services is that they lack our brain's capacity for emotion. Following their programs to the byte, they invest your money according to well-established principles that have been proven to grow money over time without taking undue risk. Unlike human investors, the software doesn't freak out when markets crash and it doesn't get greedy when tech stocks or mortgage-based investments go on a tear. Software is unemotional when it comes to rebalancing, even if it means buying what everyone is selling and selling what everyone is buying. Software is always at the office, waiting for you to check in, and it never has an attitude.

These online, software-based investing services are not completely outside the reach of our emotions, though. With a few keystrokes, an investor can make his or her portfolio more aggressive or super-conservative. Or he can sell it all and get his money back within a few days. But they do provide investors with a way to avoid obsessing over the markets and their investments.

Likewise, advisors can be your best allies in keeping your emotions from sabotaging your success. Good advisors use their powers of persuasion to remind investors, especially in volatile times, that investing success is not about emotion, it's about math.

You may have noticed that I said a little earlier that most people aren't capable of managing their investments very well. That brings us to the rest of the population. A small percentage of people *are* capable of keeping their emotional wrecking balls sufficiently in check to invest successfully. And it really is mostly a matter of mastering your emotions. As you'll now learn, investing in and of itself really isn't very hard.

Key Points

- Our minds are powerful computers and often take shortcuts to manage the mass of data that we must process.
- These shortcuts often make consumers susceptible to salesmanship, where we make decisions based on comfort rather than quality.
- Sales is an art in and of itself. Beware of well-dressed salesmen who make your head spin with information you don't understand. A great

advisor should be able to explain anything they do in simple language.

- For a whole host of reasons, most investors are likely to be their own worst enemy, making emotional decisions rather than rational calculations about their investments.

Chapter 7

How to Be Your Own Investment Advisor

Most of us seek expert advice on any subject where we lack expertise. Said differently, most humans are lazy when it comes to matters that don't interest them, and as a result, they're often willing to simply rely on the advice of others. Amazingly, this seems to be true even in cases where we know the advice is worthless.

A 2012 study by Asian researchers shows this in all its absurdity. Undergraduate college students in Thailand and Singapore were asked to place bets on the results of coin flips. Coin flips are, of course, completely random, a fact that every adult should understand. To researchers' surprise, some participants actually paid for third-party predictions about the coin-toss outcomes. What's more amazing is that, if the predictions turned out to be "correct," the students were likely to pay even more for more predictions—and to place larger bets on subsequent coin tosses! Humans want to believe they can gain an edge when it comes to making money. This is true in horse racing, gambling in Vegas, and investing.

A recent column in *The Economist* magazine suggested another reason investors might insist on relying on others for advice. Following someone else's advice ensures that we'll have someone other than ourselves to blame if our investments crash.

The truth, however, is that, as much as we might feel compelled to hire an advisor, we may not need to. This is simply because the basic elements of investing successfully are just not that difficult.

Notice that I said the *elements* of investing aren't difficult. Actually executing these elements successfully *is* difficult, and we'll talk about why in a moment. Many people think financial advisors and other professional investors possess some sort of unique ability that they don't. But the truth is that investing isn't magic; it isn't rocket science. This is not to say that there aren't outliers such as Warren Buffett or David Einhorn. But such folks are noteworthy for the same reason airline crashes are noteworthy—they are rare. The elements of successful long-term investing are about as difficult as putting together a piece of IKEA furniture and tightening its screws every now and then.

As with assembling that piece of furniture, investing involves a series of 11 steps that you simply have to complete in the proper order. Below, you'll find a framework for the basic investing process. It's the same set of steps that a good advisor would use. And it's all based on well-established science and is easily replicated.

1. **Know where you are starting from** with respect to your assets, liabilities, and goals (have a balance sheet). As the old saying goes, "How

do you know how to get where you are going if you don't know where you are?"

2. **Identify your goal(s)**. A key to successful investing is to invest toward a goal. Your goal, whether it's paying for college, paying off debt, saving for a holiday, or retiring with the ability to maintain a comfortable lifestyle, is the true north on your investment compass.

3. **Determine the cost of your goal**. The math for paying off debt or saving for something in the future is easier than calculating how much you'll need to retire, but the cost of any goal can easily be determined through Monte Carlo simulation, which is available through numerous sources. Monte Carlo analysis requires the use of software to analyze probable investment outcomes under numerous scenarios. Something as complex as calculating the cost of retirement requires only a few pieces of data, including how much cash flow (adjusted for taxes and inflation) will be required to enjoy your lifestyle, the number of years until you retire, and your current age. An obvious goal is to avoid outliving your money, so it's best to project living into your 90s or even 100.

To properly calculate the amount you need to save and ultimately earn on your investments, everything will need to be adjusted for inflation. Annual inflation of 2.5 percent is the long-term historical average, but you may want to use 3 percent or even greater considering the current environment. In the end, it's best to *plan for the worst and hope for the best* than to experience the inverse.

4. **Do some subtraction**. Subtract assets and income that will be available at your target date (say, the date you plan to retire) from other sources of assets. These sources can include, for example, workplace retirement plans, Social Security, and any ongoing royalties or rents. This gives you your "magic number"—the amount you'll need in your do-it-yourself retirement investment account in order to pay for your goal.

5. **Identify what you'll contribute or save**. Your investment portfolio will grow from both market appreciation and any continuing contributions. You can control only the contributions, so you'll need to figure out your initial investment and any ongoing amount you'll be adding to the account.

6. **Determine your required rate of return**. That's the rate that will get you to your magic number by your "deadline." By simulating the potential outcomes within a reasonable range, then repeating that process thousands of times, Monte Carlo simulation can tell you the minimum return required in order to have a high likelihood of meeting your spending objectives.

7. **Know what you can handle**. If your required return when considering taxes, inflation, time horizon, and what you have today is between 1 and 6 percent after-tax, then a normal diversified portfolio should be able to meet your goals. If your requirements are less than 1 percent or greater than 6 percent, then risk tolerance is going to play a bigger role. Therefore, you'll need to understand your tolerance for risk—or period to period changes in value.

8. **Diversify**. If you subscribe to what's called Modern Portfolio Theory, then it's important to understand that you won't need to determine your asset allocation, as the makeup of the portfolio will be heavily determined by the desired return.

9. **Choose your investments**. For the most part, the typical individual can be successful by selecting exchange-traded funds (ETFs) or index mutual funds. These investments are "passively managed," meaning that they are designed to match the market—or segments of it—rather than beat it. "Actively managed" funds, on the other hand, involve active buying and selling of stocks and bonds in an attempt to beat the market. Passively managed funds are generally more cost efficient and tax efficient than actively managed funds. They're simple to use and fully liquid, meaning you can cash out quickly if you need to. However, if picking actively managed funds or trying to beat the market averages is important to you, then finding a good advisor can be helpful. (Read on to learn more about how I see the active-versus-passive investing debate.) Be certain to understand, though, how your advisor is compensated and what tools he or she has to help select mutual funds, managers, and hedge funds. Conflicts in compensation can quickly erode any advantage that you might hope to gain. Note: When working

with some of the wealthiest families in the world, my suggested expectation is that if active management adds an extra 1 percent to returns after fees and taxes, then we should consider ourselves successful.

10. **Do routine maintenance**. Over the years, your investment mix will need to be trimmed or added to. Most importantly, it will need to be rebalanced. This housekeeping is extremely important and can add 0.5 to 1.0 percent of additional annual return. Ignore it, and the ability to make your magic number could be compromised. Here's a simplified example: Suppose you determine that your portfolio should comprise two fundamental types of investments, or "asset classes." Say you decide that those asset classes should be stocks and bonds, and that 60 percent of the money should be in stocks, 40 percent in bonds. Then suppose that, even though you start with the 60/40 split, your stocks do so well that their share of the pie grows from 60 to 70 percent. Your job as a rebalancer will be to sell enough stock and buy enough bonds to restore the original 60/40

ratio. I call this the Robin Hood Rule: You should always *rob from the rich (asset classes) and give to the poor (asset classes)*. Resist the temptation to stay with a rising asset class. The reason is that asset classes "cycle." While the stocks in the S&P 500 or emerging market indexes may have been the "hot dots" for the past few years, chances are that they will cool off and regress to their average return over time. So keep your bets spread around according to your original plan. That's what rebalancing is. And, besides, if you can earn an extra 0.5 percent or more just by doing this, that's basically the proverbial *free lunch*.

11. **Get help if you need it**. If all of this seems to be too much math or makes your brain hurt, there are numerous resources available to help and more and more being released each day. Otherwise, you can hire a financial planner for a few hours to do all the analysis for you—without an ongoing commitment.

Remember, your goal is simply to choose investments that, when combined together, are likely to generate your required rate of return *over a long period of time* with the minimum required risk. You don't need to make brilliant calls. You don't have to generate rock-star manager returns. You simply need to be *in it to win it*. Stay invested. Stay diversified. And rebalance. It's that simple. The odds are stacked in your favor.

And always, always remember your objective: to achieve the magic number that you need to pay for your retirement, or your kids' college, or whatever you've got your eye on. As long as you're on track to be able to pay for your goal, all is well—go and enjoy your life.

You don't need to be Warren Buffett to handle your own investing. Trust me; the advisor industry isn't exactly filled with Mensa[1] members. And if thousands of advisors can do it, the odds are that you can too.

---

[1] Mensa is the largest and oldest high IQ society in the world. It is a nonprofit organization open to people who score at the ninety-eighth percentile or higher on a standardized, supervised IQ or other approved intelligence test.

These Terms Are Your Friends

- Modern Portfolio Theory (MPT): An academic investing theory aimed at maximizing expected portfolio returns for a given amount of risk. MPT helps investors choose a mix of investments that are likely to provide the returns they seek with the lowest amount of risk. It's used by investors, advisors, and investing software to determine which investments to include in a portfolio.

- Asset Allocation: Asset allocation refers to the proportion of stocks, bonds, and cash (or very safe investments such as Treasury bills) and types of each within a portfolio. The success of your portfolio has far more to do with asset allocation than with the individual stocks, bonds, and other investments you choose. Academic studies show that asset allocation accounts for more than 90 percent of the positive performance of an investment portfolio.

- Monte Carlo simulation: A computer simulation used to analyze probable investment outcomes under numerous scenarios that involve different rates of interest, inflation, taxes, and so on. Monte Carlo simulations help investors build portfolios that are able to withstand the uncertainty that's always present in the real world. They're often used to help investors invest for retirement.
- Diversification: The science of mixing a variety of investments within a portfolio in order to achieve desired returns with the least risk. It's the opposite of putting all your eggs in one basket. Studies have shown that properly diversifying across 25 to 30 stocks provides significant protection against risk.

Don't Let Costs Mug Your Returns

One of the biggest mistakes that investors make is to focus on returns and treat costs as an afterthought.

But paying close attention to costs is critical. The less you pay in transaction fees to buy a stock, the bigger your profit once you sell your appreciated shares. And the lower the management fees within your mutual fund or exchange-traded fund, the greater your potential profit down the road. It's a simple concept, but investors often become so fixated on returns that they ignore what they're paying to get those returns. A simple example illustrates how even a small difference in cost can make a significant difference in return.

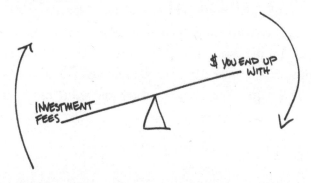

INVESTMENT FEES

$ YOU END UP WITH

Let's say you invest $10,000, on which you'll earn 5 percent a year—not counting management fees. Before fees, you will have a total after 10 years of $16,288.95.

Now suppose you pay a management fee of 1 percent per year: In that case, your effective return will be not 5 percent but 4 percent—and your return will be slashed by $1,486.50 for a total return of $14,802.44.

Now suppose your management fee is higher—say 2 percent. That 2 percent fee brings your effective rate of return to 3 percent and will shrink your 10-year return by $2,849.78, to just $13,439.16. As a percentage, this is meaningful and, in reality, makes a very large difference in your quest to achieve your goals.

The good news for investors is that they have access to investments with low fees; these are the index mutual funds and exchange-traded funds. These products provide diversification at costs that are significantly lower than many alternatives. Below is a guide to the average costs associated with different types of investments.

Individual Stocks and Bonds

By assembling your own portfolio, you avoid management costs—because you're the manager. But you don't avoid trading costs. And trading costs can add up quickly, even if you use a discount broker. Remember that every stock, bond, or other investment that you buy, you'll eventually sell—which means you'll pay two transaction fees for each of your holdings. Nowadays, the least expensive route is via an online broker where transactions are typically $10 or less per trade. However, this approach begs questions, such as how many trades you'll need to make, whether you'll be able to properly diversify, and whether you'll be able to stay on top of buying and selling securities when it's necessary.

Actively Managed Mutual Funds

Mutual funds bundle a number of expenses together, calculate a total annual fee, and subtract that amount from your account. You never even need to be bothered with the bill, regardless of how large it may be—that decision is made for you. The largest of active funds' expenses is the fee paid to their managers to do the investing within the fund. Other costs range from recordkeeping to legal expenses to accounting fees—and many funds include in their charges a marketing fee. The average actively managed fund's expense ratio—or total fees charged to its investors—is around 1.4 percent. That means you'll pay $14 per year for every $1,000 you invest. The expense ratio doesn't include the costs of actually buying shares of the fund. But because many mutual funds contain a diverse mix of stocks, these fees work out to less than they'd be if you bought the same collection of stocks yourself.

Index Mutual Funds

Index mutual funds are a cheaper way to get a diversified basket of stocks or bonds. When you invest in actively managed mutual funds, you're hiring a team of professionals to do the management. This team—the lead manager, his assistants, and a support team of analysts and others—are constantly looking for opportunities to buy and sell the fund's holdings in order to beat the market. Index funds don't involve any of that frenetic activity. These "passive" investments are designed to match the market—or certain slices of it—rather than beat it. Index funds invest in lists of stocks or bonds that rarely change, such as the stocks in the Standard & Poor's 500 Index or the Barclays U.S. Aggregate Bond Index. The average expense ratio for index funds is around 0.75 percent, but can be as low as 0.007 percent.

Index mutual funds—and exchange-traded funds— are especially attractive to do-it-yourself investors because they provide a simple, cheap way to buy diverse chunks of the market. Want to buy exposure to all the companies in the S&P 500, for example? It's as simple as choosing one of the many funds that track that index.

Exchange-Traded Funds

ETFs are the younger siblings of index mutual funds. Like their older kin, they give investors a simple way to invest in a broad slice of the market. Since their introduction in the early 1990s, ETFs have steadily eaten into mutual funds' market share. Part of the reason is that they can be cheaper than even index mutual funds—provided that you make a large enough investment. ETFs track market indexes and the broader the index they track, the cheaper they tend to be. In general, ETFs often charge lower management fees than index mutual funds; the reasons are largely technical and have to do with the way shares of the respective products are created. The average ETF carries an expense ratio of 0.44 percent.

There's an important caveat, however. When you buy additional shares of mutual funds, you typically don't have to pay trading costs, particularly if you've set up regularly scheduled purchases. On the other hand, you must pay a brokerage commission each time you buy ETF shares—and those sales charges add up fast.

Hedge Funds

Hedge funds have often been likened to mutual funds for rich people—and they sure charge like that is what they are. Open to investors with high incomes and at least $1 million of net worth, they're known for charging "2 and 20"—a 2 percent annual management fee and 20 percent of profits. In their attempt to generate high or consistent returns, hedge fund managers exercise far more latitude than mutual fund managers. Because some funds borrow money to pump up their investment bets, hedge funds are riskier than the overall market.

No investment is free. But paying attention to costs is worth it. When you pay the lowest possible fees, you leave more money in your account to compound over the years—and that can make a big difference in the long run. Think of it this way: When you choose which investments to buy, you're also choosing whether to maximize the money in your account or to help pay for a manager's latest sports car. If you examine the latest entrants onto the Forbes 400 list of wealthiest Americans, you will notice that over the last 10 to 20 years one of the fastest growing industries is the hedge fund industry. Not that many of these folks haven't earned that net worth, but think of the many who have tried and failed while investors foot the bill.

How to Win the Game by Not Playing

Investing doesn't have to be complicated. The simplest way to do it—which also happens to be the least expensive, most tax-efficient, most worry-free, and historically most successful—is known as index investing.

To understand index investing, also known as passive investing, let's first take a look at its sexier twin, active investing. To those in the active camp, investing means searching for stocks or other securities that an investment manager believes can perform better than the broad market or asset class (as defined by an index[2]). Active investors believe they can beat the market by working harder, being shrewder, and finding opportunities faster than other investors.

---

[2]An index is a theoretical "basket" of securities designed to represent, or mirror, a broad market or a portion of the market.

Based on the long-term data, the vast majority of investors are kidding themselves. Let's start with the *do-it-yourselfers*. If you're an amateur investor using an active approach, you're likely to end up like a fly on a windshield over the long term. The only thing worse than losing money out of the gate may be to win consistently for a period of time—this can lead one to become overconfident in their ability, just like a gambler on a hot streak in Vegas. We saw this in the late 1990s as large-cap and tech stocks rapidly outpaced the broad market. Active investing is a full-time job, not a moonlighting gig. And, while an occasional genius has the ability to see things that others don't see, I challenge you to find the next Warren Buffett or Peter Lynch.

Even professional investors, supported by teams of dedicated researchers who eat, drink, and breathe stocks and bonds, have enormous difficulty just matching the market's results, much less beating them. In 2011, about 84 percent of actively managed U.S. stock mutual funds lagged the indexes representing the market segment they invest in, according to Standard & Poor's. Unfortunately, 2011 was not an anomaly. And that's not even taking into consideration the many active funds that have done poorly over the years and eventually gone out of business (a phenomenon called "survivorship bias").

Active investors' results get really ugly when you factor in costs and taxes. Many a *do-it-yourselfer* has opened a discount brokerage account, started buying and selling stocks, and achieved what at first glance appears to be decent results. Decent, that is, until the fees for buying and selling stocks are factored in. Brokerage fees, even at discount brokerages, have an uncanny way of transforming great trading returns into mediocre ones, and mediocre returns into train wrecks. Remember, it's not how much you earn in the market; it's how much that winds up in your pocket that counts.

What about investing in actively managed mutual funds? Actively managed funds provide professional management and diversification. But in addition to the fact that they usually lag the market, their costs—layer after layer of them—can be ruinous.

The first layer of mutual fund costs can come when you buy shares. Traditionally, brokers have charged an up-front sales commission of up to 5 percent of your initial investment; although that number has come down over the last decade. That bloated fee effectively carves 5 percent off your first year's performance (assuming it's positive performance). The result: Your fund will have to significantly outperform over the ensuing years to make you a net profit. As investors have started to catch on to the up-front fee, fund companies have concocted alternative commission models. These clever arrangements let investors pay commissions in increments over time, or when they sell their shares. Trust me, this can be just as bad—and in some cases worse—than paying up-front fees.

Understanding Fund Fees

Mutual fund shares are sold through brokers as A, B, and C, and other shares. Though each "share class" charges a different mix of sales commission and annual management fees, the bottom line is that buying loaded shares this way can cost you a bundle.

A shares: Also known as front-loaded shares, they usually feature fat upfront fees, of up to 5 percent on average, and lower management fees. Investors can often get discounts for larger investment amounts.

B   shares: "Back-end-loaded" shares usually have no upfront sales charge but do feature higher ongoing fees. Plus, they impose a charge on investors who sell in the early years. After several years, B shares typically convert to A shares, meaning their management expenses decline.

C shares: These "level-load" shares have no up-front or back-end load, but do have high ongoing expenses. Unlike B shares, Cs rarely convert to As, meaning they'll stay expensive as long as you own them.

The truth is that there's little reason to pay commissions at all: A great number of no-load funds are available without sales charges through advisors or through no-transaction-fee supermarkets such as Charles Schwab.

The next layer of costs is known as the expense ratio, or the cost of running a fund and marketing it. The expense ratio, naturally, is paid for by the funds' investors, typically to the tune of 1.5 percent per year of invested assets.

A fund's sales commission and expense ratio together can seriously hobble your investment results. Suppose you invest $100,000 in a stock mutual fund. You pay a 5 percent commission and a 1.5 percent expense ratio, and your return is 10 percent a year. After a decade, fees and foregone earnings will have sucked up more than $47,000—about 18 percent of your gains.

But wait: There can still be more layers of costs! The next comes in the form of trading fees. The typical active mutual fund manager sells many of the stocks in the portfolio within a year's time. This high level of "turnover" results in trading costs that Vanguard founder, John Bogle, estimates shave 1 percent a year from fund investors' results. That's on top of commissions and expense ratios. In fact, many funds charge you for the privilege of selling to you through something called a 12b-1 fee.[3] On top of all

---

[3] *12b-1 Fee* is a fee used to pay for a mutual fund's distribution costs. It is often used as a commission to brokers for selling the fund. The amount, which can be as high as 75 basis points for commissions and 25 basis points for service fees, is taken from a fund's returns.

that, frequent selling of winners in actively managed portfolios is likely to result in more capital gains taxes.

It's no wonder that Bogle, who is revered as an educator and advocate for investors, has spent decades pounding home his powerful message: "Costs matter." They do!

For most people, the wisest approach to investing is to embrace two simple precepts: Be patient, and be passive. First, be patient by holding your investments for the long term and giving them a real chance to appreciate. Second, be passive. Not by doing nothing, but by investing in a way that lets you ride the currents of the stock market rather than fighting them.

The best passive investing strategy is to simply buy a diversified portfolio of broad-market index mutual funds or ETFs and to hold them for the long term, rebalancing as appropriate. By buying shares of a fund that tracks the S&P 500 index or Wilshire 5000 Total Market Index, an investor can own sufficient exposure to the U.S. stock market, or darned close to it. The same is true for all other asset classes appropriate in a portfolio.

Why does it make sense to do that? First, because investing in a wide array of companies across many different industries is the classic way to limit your risk—it's the antithesis of putting all your eggs in one basket. More importantly, patiently betting on the overall stock market to rise over the long term is far more profitable than making short-term bets on individual companies. I would argue that the *only* free lunch in investing is diversification.

For proof, just compare the historical performance of index mutual funds with the performance of actively managed funds. As Princeton professor Burton G. Malkiel has pointed out, index funds "have regularly produced rates of return exceeding those of active managers by close to two percentage points."

Investing in the entire market is the equivalent of betting on capitalism as a whole. Yes, the markets might rise one year and fall the next, and any given stock might soar one day and crash the next. But over the long term, trusting the market has been richly rewarded. Consider that between October 1, 1928, and October 1, 2012, the Dow Jones Industrial Average—an index of 30 major U.S. stocks—has risen more than 5,500 percent.

Index funds and ETFs allow you to invest in the broad market at very little expense. Vanguard's S&P 500 fund, known as the Vanguard 500 Index fund, is the best deal out there; its expense ratio is an ultra-cheap 5 basis points or 0.005 percent.

Another great reason to own a broad-market index fund: They are extremely tax-efficient. Why? Because an index fund invests in a fixed list of stocks, buying and selling only on the rare occasions when a new stock is added to their benchmark index. The infrequency of selling ensures that very little tax liability is created. Furthermore, index funds' static nature means that trading costs tend to range between negligible and nothing. Sales are more often triggered by withdrawals by investors from the fund that exceed contributions, and can lead to some tax impact, but typically this is nominal other than in periods like late 2008 when there was a mass exodus from equity assets.

Index investing is as profitable as it is simple. But human nature being what it is, investors and investment product manufacturers have found ways to make it complex and counterproductive. Since Vanguard introduced the first index fund more than 35 years ago, thousands of index funds have appeared, along with their offshoot, exchange-traded funds. The funds have focused on narrower and narrower slices of the market, to the point where we now have funds that let you invest in areas as esoteric as natural gas or corn and it's getting even more specific each year.

I'd strongly advise you to stick with much broader index funds. One reason among many: The narrower your investment focus, the greater your risk. Folks who are eager to focus their bets on the *can't-miss* sector of the day should do a little historical research. Remember the dot-com bubble of the late 1990s and early 2000s? The real-estate bubble of the late 2000s? Investors in those sectors thought they were pretty smart—until the bubbles inevitably popped and vaporized their money.

Indexing is a proven route to long-term investing success. But it has another benefit that's too-often overlooked. Committing to patient, passive investing can remove a massive amount of anxiety and stress from your life. Passive investors aren't constantly comparing their performance to the market or to other investors' results. They aren't pouring energy into finding the hot new stock or actively managed mutual fund or sector ETF. They aren't obsessing over finding needles in haystacks.

Passive investors are free to focus their energy on areas that, frankly, can make them happier and more fulfilled than the stock market can. Whether it's career, family relationships, hobbies, or volunteering, passive investors have more time and energy for it.

Now, I'll admit that patient, passive investing can seem dull to some folks. So if you need short-term investment thrills, then by all means go ahead and play the market—but do it with just a sliver of your money. A good rule of thumb is to set aside no more than 5 percent of your investable assets as "play money." Just don't be surprised if you lose some of it.

Life Insurance in a Nutshell

There's an old saying that life insurance is sold, not bought. This is the case because most people don't get excited about the idea of buying something they will never enjoy. Occasionally sold as an investment because of its tax benefits, insurance—as a general rule—is insurance.

Insurance is often used to provide liquidity to replace the income or economic value of a key person (often a spouse) lost to an untimely death. It can also be used to preserve an estate, or generate liquidity to pay estate taxes in the event of a large but illiquid estate. For this discussion, I'll touch on the more common use of insurance, creating an estate.

Life insurance, while not exciting to discuss or fun to own, provides immense utility for a family that has not yet accumulated the necessary assets and/or liquidity to sustain the loss of an earner or replace the care of a parent.

Sadly, I've seen too many situations where an unexpected death turns a family's financial situation upside down, adding fear to the pain of an untimely passing. In its simplest form, life insurance can create a pool of assets from which to generate cash flow in the event of death. It can enable survivors to pay off debt; it can help send your kids to college. Life insurance can keep a personal tragedy from compounding into a personal and financial tragedy.

Just as with investing or choosing a financial advisor, you should be educated and empowered when buying insurance. Accordingly, let's clear away one of the biggest uncertainties people have about insurance: How much does one need? You won't be surprised to learn that there are lots of unscrupulous insurance brokers out there, and they are all too happy to sell you far more coverage than is necessary. And since there are lots of different commission structures and differing levels of quality among carriers, the choices are exhausting. In many cases, consumers sense this and overcompensate by buying too little insurance. Here's a simple way, in six steps, to calculate how much insurance you should actually buy.

1. Figure out how much money the surviving spouse would need, in today's dollars, to live a comfortable lifestyle. Don't include taxes.
2. Multiply that number by 33.
3. Add to that the present value of major obligations (college tuition, mortgage payoff if desired, and so on).

4. Add any outstanding debt that you might want to extinguish (and which is not factored into #1 above).

5. Subtract your current liquid savings (cash, savings, stocks, bonds, etc.). If you want to be conservative, exclude retirement savings, since there are restrictions on when those monies can be withdrawn.

6. The sum of these numbers is the amount of insurance you should purchase.

The next question you'll ask is what kind of insurance to buy. There are two major categories to choose from: term life insurance and permanent insurance. Term insurance gives you a specific, agreed-upon benefit for a specific amount of time. If you buy a 10-year, $500,000 policy, for example, your beneficiary will receive $500,000 if you die during the 10 years the policy is in force. The premium you pay is essentially the cost of the risk that you die early. You can typically buy term insurance for up to 20 years with a guaranteed level premium. After the "term" expires, your policy premiums can increase dramatically, particularly if you are not able to secure a new policy due to a health issue that would render you uninsurable. Like auto insurance, your term coverage ends and you don't get any money back. The joke in the industry is that you only "win"—meaning the death benefit is paid out—if you die.

Permanent insurance is different and comes in many flavors. Permanent policies offer death benefits, just as term policies do. But they also feature a "savings account," otherwise known as "cash value." These policies are significantly more expensive over the short term (less than 15 or 20 years) than term insurance. This is because that extra premium funds a "savings account" within the policy to fund future premium payments. And if you live as long as you're supposed to, you can tap into that cash value.

If you've made premium payments for long enough, you'll likely recoup the cost of those premiums and may even come out ahead.

Because there are so many variables involved in choosing term or permanent, it can be difficult to decide which way to go. Here's the general rule I give my clients:

If you want life insurance for up to 15 years, you're better off with a term life policy. Want coverage for more than 15 years? That's the point at which paying the higher premiums for permanent insurance may make more sense.

And, at the risk of really oversimplifying, when considering the investment aspect of insurance—despite what anyone tries to sell you—insurance is the equivalent of a municipal bond with a lottery ticket attached to it. In other words, at normal life expectancy you could have put the same amount of money into high-quality bonds and earned about the same return. However, if the insured dies early, the return obviously increases dramatically (although I don't think anyone will feel like they won the lottery).

Now, when you're ready to shop for insurance, please don't go to the first insurance broker you come across. You can buy term from many companies, and the quality of the company is far less relevant than if you purchase a permanent policy. Note: There are numerous websites that can do the shopping for you. If you want to consider a permanent policy, try to buy from a top-quality (rated AA or better; preferably AAA) company.

Software-Powered Investing

In recent years, sites that function almost as virtual investment advisors have been proliferating. For a low fee, these software-based investment services use the information you provide about goals, time frame, and risk tolerance to invest your money in a diversified portfolio of low-cost index-oriented mutual funds and exchange-traded funds, and even handle the automatic rebalancing for you.

Such sites have won rave reviews, some of them from unlikely sources such as Nick Shalek. From 2005 to 2008, Shalek was part of the team that managed Yale University's $20-billion endowment. Yale's investment performance—an average annual return of 11.8 percent through the 10 years ending in mid-2009—made a cult hero of chief investment officer David Swensen. Advisors and professional investors have emulated his "Yale Model," which calls for broad diversification and a heavy focus on stocks, hedge funds, and private equity. Suffice it to say that the Yale Model is definitely not an automated software program.

Yet Shalek is among the fans of these programs. In a recent article on the widely followed site TechCrunch, he described software as "better at investing than 99 percent of active investors." By "active investors," Shalek was referring to humans—specifically investors who buy and sell stocks or other investments based on changes in their prices. The "software" he referred to, meanwhile, executes a "passive" investing strategy such as what was mentioned previously. Passive investors typically buy index funds or index ETFs, use careful research to create a diversified portfolio of investments, and hold their investments regardless of short-term price swings. Passive investors have faith that, over the long run, markets will rise and reward their patience.

Why is Shalek so high on software-based investing for 99 percent of us? In a nutshell, he likes this approach because it cuts out the human weaknesses and foibles that so often lead to trouble. Software, he points out, isn't greedy or fearful. It isn't irrational. And it never loses interest in doing its job. And successful investing is an ongoing job—something that countless do-it-yourselfers have failed to recognize. Finally, software is inexpensive; for one thing, it "doesn't have a vacation home to pay for," Shalek cheekily notes:

> Unlike us (or our investment advisors), software doesn't need to be compensated for spending time investing. It brings the marginal cost of investing much closer to zero, so it doesn't care whether you have $10,000 to invest, or $10 million. And software doesn't have conflicts of interest or look for ways to create and hide fees. It doesn't

rent fancy office space or use soft dollars to buy bloated research services. Today's software-based services enable you to invest far more cheaply than was possible even 10 years ago.

Software-based investing is a new field, and time will tell if the pioneers in the field attract enough business to succeed and survive. (By the way, these companies' novelty shouldn't discourage you from using them: Assets that you place in accounts with them are typically held by independent custodians and are insured by the Securities Investor Protection Corporation, just as is the case with human advisors.)

I believe online, software-based investing is here to stay. It's a simple and effective solution and its costs are rock-bottom. Plus, it doesn't require a large initial investment, as many advisors do. But to me, what's most intriguing about the new offerings is that they do what almost no human can—take emotion out of investing. (For full disclosure, I personally invested in Betterment.com because I believe they are well-poised to serve typical investors at a very low cost.)

Math First, Emotion Second

The elements of investing are simple. So why have so many people screwed it up, again and again, throughout history? The short answer is emotion. Humans are emotional creatures, and when it comes to investing, emotion is the enemy.

Nowhere are humans' primal emotions of fear and greed more fully on display than in the investing arena. We overreact to bad news, selling at exactly the wrong time. We smell the chance to make a killing or follow the pack, arriving late to the party, and we buy in—just before a crash.

Many do-it-yourselfers start investing with the best of intentions. They swear to maintain a long-term outlook, to stick to their plan, to be rational. But it typically isn't long before our primal emotions appear and run roughshod over our sensibility; our discipline evaporates, and we proceed to wreak havoc on our portfolios.

Some small percentage of people can keep their primal emotions in check—these are the Warren Buffetts of the world. Most of the rest of us, however, are terrible investment advisors. We would never knowingly hire someone like ourselves to invest our money, at any price.

Why You (Probably) Still Need a Financial Advisor

The truth is that the percentage of investors who can invest by the numbers and avoid all the emotional pitfalls along the way is tiny—I'd guess 10 percent of the investing population—at most. For the other 90 percent or so, hiring an advisor can be a great investment.

Good advisors earn their money during times of market extremes. In the late 1990s, they kept clients' greed from wreaking havoc by steering them away from overloading on tech stocks. In the 2008 crash, the best advisors persuaded their clients to stay the course—to avoid selling out and locking in losses. The best advisors are strong when their clients turn wobbly. When clients lose perspective, good advisors remind them that they're on a long journey and that true north is still true north and that sticking with the plan will get them there—that despite the ups and downs of the business cycle, nobody has repealed capitalism and its potential rewards for investors.

Good advisors do their utmost to talk clients out of borrowing too much against their home—or buying more home than they can afford. They encourage debt reduction and deliver the message to clients that they need to live within their means. And they help clients understand the risk of poor decisions with simple "pay now or pay later" examples.

The best advisors can also provide critical tax advice that can be of enormous benefit to clients. Tax-savvy advisors and advisor teams can help clients keep more of their wealth while alive and pass more of it along to their heirs when they die. As the saying goes, "It's not what you earn, it's what you keep."

Key Points

It's not only possible to be your own investment advisor, it's damned easy. There is one giant thing that often gets in the way—a lack of discipline.

- Core elements of successful planning:
  - Know what you have (balance sheet and cash flows) and what you need (goals).
  - Use math to understand how much risk you must take or how long you have to work/save.

- Be realistic with respect to gauging inflation, how much you spend, how much you can save, and how long you plan on working. Be conservative with the length of your possible life expectancy (assume you're going to live to be 100 years old).
- Be honest with yourself about how much volatility you can handle. If you panic at the wrong time, the penalty can be enormous.
- *Diversify, diversify, diversify!* (And that doesn't mean spreading your Apple stock out over three accounts!)
- Choose your underlying investments (ETFs, mutual funds, asset managers), but remember that this is the least important of all your decisions.
- Rebalance.
- Get help if you need it!

Chapter 8

Choosing an Advisor: Know What You Don't Know

Identifying and selecting your financial advisor is almost as important as selecting your surgeon (remember Chapter 1?). Unfortunately, as I've repeatedly pointed out, when it comes to evaluating an advisor, *most of us don't know what we don't know.*

How well you interview the key professionals in your life can certainly dictate the quality of the outcome. But how can you tell a good attorney from a mediocre attorney or, for that matter, a good investment advisor from a bad one?

At the very least, lawyers and physicians can initially be screened by the quality of their schooling. Did they go to Harvard for medical or law school, or did they graduate from a correspondence school? Medical and legal professionals also have annual continuing education requirements and state licensing. None of this guarantees that you'll hire the best lawyer or doctor, but it's definitely a good start.

Unfortunately, as we learned in Chapter 5, the barrier to entry into the wealth advisory profession is negligible, at best. There is no formal curriculum or degree that signifies expertise and/or professionalism. Pass a test, hang a shingle, and you're in business. Just add water and *poof*—you're an instant financial advisor. Clearly, this isn't the state of the entire industry. There are certain individuals from every segment of the financial advisory business who are capable of serving your needs. However, until the industry raises the bar of competence, requiring an appropriate level of skill and duty from people calling themselves wealth advisors—or until the equivalent of a "Good Housekeeping Seal of Approval" is launched for advisors—you're on your own.

But you have an important advantage: You're reading this book. By doing so, you've already empowered yourself with knowledge about how the industry works and the different kinds of advisors vying for your business. You already know how to narrow your search—by initially ruling out brokers, bank-based advisors, insurance salesmen, and fee-only financial planners (for a review of advisors to avoid and why, see Chapters 2, 3, and 4). You've learned that limiting your search to independent RIAs will give you the best chance to find an advisor who is not only qualified but is more likely to be on your side in word and deed.

If you've arrived at the point that you've decided to engage an advisor to assist you on your financial journey, you should know that you have a great deal of power, and it lies very simply in *asking the right questions*. In fact, asking informed questions of prospective advisors may prove to be one of the best investments that you can make in your financial success.

We'll get to the questions you should ask in a moment. First, however, you should understand that these questions are rooted in a set of three core principles that all advisors should uphold.

Core Principles

1. Duty—Your advisor should adhere to the highest level of duty and loyalty to clients, always putting your interests ahead of his or her own.
2. Safeguards—Your advisor should make every effort to keep clients' assets safe from fraud and keep client information private.
3. Professionalism—Your advisor should operate his or her business according to the highest standards of professionalism in the industry.

These principles are easy to understand in the abstract. But how do you know whether an advisor abides by them? That's where an advisor questionnaire comes in. The questions at the end of this chapter are based in fact, not emotion. Thus, you should expect factual answers—most of which will be verifiable through public disclosure documents and other information sources. Remember, choosing an advisor based on facts rather than emotion is a powerful way to get beyond sales pitches and into the substance of what an advisor has to offer.

You Are the Family CEO

Remember, when you hire an advisor, you're handing someone an enormous and important responsibility. He or she should come to know your financial situation better than just about anyone in your life. Choosing the right person may not guarantee your financial success, but choosing the wrong one could prove catastrophic. So before hiring your advisor, this person or firm should be made to answer tough questions. Is this uncomfortable? You bet it is. However, you are the CEO of your family affairs, and you need to think like the *big boss* making a high-level hire. If a prospective team member can't give straightforward and believable answers to your tough, direct questions, then they don't have the right stuff for the job. So be rigorous in the interview process. It may well save you a lot of pain down the road.

Truly qualified, professional advisors will welcome these questions. Their pride in offering a consumer-friendly service will come through in their answers. As for those who are in the business more for themselves than for you, your questions may make them squirm. If that's the case, take their discomfort as a red flag and thank them for their time. *Bring in the next candidate, please!*

Speaking of the next candidate, I strongly urge you to interview *at least* three advisors before hiring one. If you're not comparing multiple options before making a commitment—whether you're hiring a brain surgeon, buying a car, or engaging an advisor—you are doing yourself a disservice. And as you'll see in the questions that follow, some aspects of an advisor's practice can only be evaluated by comparing them with his competition.

Keep our core principles in mind when interviewing potential advisors. Remember, you're determining whether the advisor measures up in three distinct areas:

1. His or her dedication to clients before profits.
2. His or her commitment to safeguarding your assets and your privacy.
3. His or her professional qualifications.

Bring copies of pages 193–204 when interviewing your advisors, then decode their answers beginning on page 205.

Core Principle: DUTY—Clients before Profits

IDEALS

Your advisor adheres to the highest level of duty and loyalty to clients.

IN PLAIN ENGLISH: *The client's interests always come first.*

Your advisor adheres to the highest level of appropriateness and care for clients.

IN PLAIN ENGLISH: *Clients should be treated with care. Advisors cannot control the markets, but they can control the service!*

Your advisor meets the highest legal standard of professional conduct.

IN PLAIN ENGLISH: *As strange as it may sound, different laws apply to different types of firms and advisors. Some laws are less stringent than others. Make sure your advisor meets the highest standards. For my money, it's the fiduciary standard that reigns supreme in today's environment.*

Demonstrate a culture of compliance.

IN PLAIN ENGLISH: *Compliance isn't just following the letter of the law. It means promoting and rewarding ethical behavior among all staff members.*

Avoid conflicts of interest created by compensation.

IN PLAIN ENGLISH: *Advisors should be paid by clients, not product providers or any one other than the client.*

What to Ask

---

1. Can you describe your typical client?

A. Do you have a unique expertise or a specific focus on certain types of clients (e.g., retirees, doctors, small business owners)? If you had to identify one type of client that is the largest percentage of your client base who would it be?

B. What is your average account size (mean)? What is your median account size? What is your total Assets Under Management (AUM) / Assets Under Advisement (AUA)? How many clients do you have?

THINGS TO LOOK FOR OR REVIEW
Client testimonials and references.

---

2. Can you describe your service profile?

A. Describe the typical service your client expects and what you deliver as standard practice. How often do they speak with an advisor and what is the advisor's level of experience?

B. Does your firm utilize technology to interface with clients? Describe the ways we can access our advisor and our information.

C. How many times per year do you meet with clients face to face? In what other forms will you communicate with us (describe)?

D. How many advisors does your firm have? How many support professionals do you have? What would my team look like?

THINGS TO LOOK FOR OR REVIEW
Review the service agreement you would have to sign. Ask to meet support staff members or anyone else you will be interfacing with on a regular basis. And, don't be afraid to ask for contract modifications, if you need them!

---

3. Will you please provide a list of all the licenses you carry?

A. Are you a licensed stockbroker? Are you a licensed insurance agent? Are you a Registered Investment Advisor? Is your firm registered with the SEC? Is your SEC registration current?

THINGS TO LOOK FOR OR REVIEW
SEC/FINRA database search (http://www.sec.gov/investor/brokers.htm).

---

4. How do you ensure that your firm remains in compliance with legal and regulatory statutes?

A. When did you last undergo an SEC audit?
B. Does your firm undergo mock audits? If yes, how often?
C. Does your firm have an outside auditor? If yes, please provide their name and contact information.
D. Does your firm have a dedicated compliance officer with no other responsibilities? If yes, please provide their resume.

THINGS TO LOOK FOR OR REVIEW
Understand their regulatory record and audit review process. Ensure that there are qualified and appropriate checks and balances to safeguard your assets.

---

5. How do you get paid?

A. How do you get paid for investments you may recommend? Do some investments you recommend pay you more than others?

B. Are you paid commissions on investments or other products (i.e., insurance) you sell? If the answer is "No," move on. However, *if the answer is "Yes" ask,*
  - "What percentage of your business is fee based versus commission based? What accounts for the difference?"
  - "Will you ever recommend commission based products for my portfolio?"

C. Are there any other forms of compensation (such as cash, trips, or other bonuses) that you may receive as a result of my business with you?

D. Does your firm receive any payments in any form from any of the mutual fund or other investment companies that you may recommend?

E. Can you be paid a flat annual fee? Can be it be an agreed-upon dollar amount per year? Can it be an agreed-upon percentage per year?

F. Do you manage any client assets yourself? If yes, how do you determine when it is time to fire yourself? Do you have any economic incentive to manage the funds yourself?

G. Is there any case where you charge clients a wealth management fee and another fee on top of that for investment products managed by your firm or any business related to your firm?

H. Aside from what I pay you, what other costs will I incur?

THINGS TO LOOK FOR OR REVIEW
Review the firm's SEC Form ADV (http://www.sec.gov/answers/formadv.htm) and check licenses, particularly insurance and brokerage. Ask about fee-sharing arrangements with vendors, mutual fund companies, or money managers. Ask about the fee structure for assets the advisor manages. Ask the advisor to break out all of the embedded costs you will pay. Double check expenses and fees against their ADV.

Your checklist:

☐ Request client testimonials and references.

☐ Review average account size. You don't want to be one of the largest or smallest clients.

☐ Comparison shop. Fees should start at 1% and go down from there. If you're only getting asset allocation and fund/manager selection services, that should cost 0.25% or less. The value of the advice should make up the difference.

☐ Review the service agreement.

☐ Interview support staff.

☐ Review the firm's ADV.

☐ Perform an SEC/FINRA database search to identify any marks on the firm or individuals' records.

☐ Review regulatory record and third-party audits, if possible.

Core Principle: SAFEGUARDS

IDEALS

Advisors should use a third-party administrator and third-party auditor, each of significant standing, for assets that cannot be held by a custodian.

IN PLAIN ENGLISH: *Checks and balances help keep your money safe.*

Separate investment management decision making (discretion) and custody.

IN PLAIN ENGLISH: *More checks and balances to help keep your money safe.*

Maintain an appropriate level of liability insurance ($5 million of coverage should be a minimum per incident).

IN PLAIN ENGLISH: *Insurance protects clients in cases where their advisor makes an error.*

Document and follow stringent privacy and employee conduct policies including employee background checks.

IN PLAIN ENGLISH: *Advisors should stand behind their values about ethics with strong and well-enforced policies.*

What to Ask

---

1. What safeguards does your firm have in place to ensure that my assets are protected from fraud?

A. Where will my assets be custodied?

B. Do you use any structures where you are deemed to have custody (e.g., limited liability companies or hedge funds) where you are the manager?

C. Do you require that any investment that is not held by an independent custodian (such as partnerships, hedge funds, or LLCs) utilize a quality, well-known accounting firm to conduct audits of these investments?

D. Do all of the funds/investments mentioned above employ a third-party administrator?

E. Will this be a discretionary relationship or will you contact me before making any changes to my portfolio?

F. Who can move money out of my account?

G. How will my accounts be titled?

H. What is your level of liability insurance and who is your liability insurance carrier?

I. How do you ensure privacy of my information? Please provide a copy of your privacy policy.

J. How do you monitor your employees' ethical conduct?

K. Have you ever had to fire an employee for unethical conduct?

THINGS TO LOOK FOR OR REVIEW
Use of a major (public company) custodian, limited use of partnership or LLC products, evidence of insurance coverage.

Your checklist:

☐ Research the custodian your prospective advisor uses. Look for a name you recognize.

☐ Ask to see third-party fund audits proving the money in funds is where they say it is. Only accept audits form well respected firms.

☐ Ask for verification of insurance coverage.

☐ Ask to see written policies for managing discretionary relationships.

☐ Ask to see written policies and procedures used to guard against fraud.

☐ Review advisor's privacy policy.

☐ Review advisor's ethics policy.

Core Principle: **PROFESSIONALISM**

IDEALS
Demonstrate robust, industry-leading business operations including continuity planning, record retention policies, and human resource practices.   IN PLAIN ENGLISH: *Healthy, thriving businesses take the time to document core activities and to mitigate business risks.*
Maintain appropriate credentials, experience, accreditation, and ongoing education.   IN PLAIN ENGLISH: *Surprisingly, there are minimal educational requirements to become a financial advisor. Top advisors seek out education and should have designations that evidence that effort.*
Manage investments objectively, with a defined process, adequate tracking, and with open architecture.   IN PLAIN ENGLISH: *Discipline is key when managing investments.*

What to Ask

---

1. What does your firm do to plan for the future?

A. What happens to my relationship if you die, are disabled, or retire? Who services my account besides you?

B. What happens to the firm if the largest shareholder dies?

THINGS TO LOOK FOR OR REVIEW
Ask to see succession planning documents, disaster recovery policies, and other relevant policies and procedures.

---

2. Can you please provide a list of your credentials and background?

A. How long have you been a financial advisor? What was your formal training?

B. What do you do to stay current?

C. What other skills do you bring to the table that can improve my family's financial condition?

D. What are the credentials of the other people working on my account?

E. What are your professional credentials and are they current?

THINGS TO LOOK FOR OR REVIEW
Ask to see advisor and staff resumes. It may even be worth confirming designations such as CFA or CFP with the issuing associations.

3. Can you explain in plain English your investment process?

A. Do you provide me with an investment policy statement? How often is it reviewed? Does it identify appropriate benchmarks for each investment so we can analyze your manager selection success? Please provide a sample.

B. Does your performance report show my returns, net of all fees? Does it illustrate each investment against an appropriate benchmark?

C. Do you use a formal investment selection process? If yes, please provide a copy. Do you rely on someone else's research? If so, who and why?

D. Do you direct any client assets to outside hedge funds or other partnership structures? If so, what are your policies and procedures for selecting these funds?

E. Do you manage any of the assets in-house?

F. If I work with you, will I have a limited number of investment choices? If so, who decides which investments are in the universe of choices?

G. How large is your investment research team?

THINGS TO LOOK FOR OR REVIEW
Ask to review a sample investment policy statement. Ask the advisor to walk you through their process for analyzing and recommending investments; as well as assessing ongoing performance. Ask to review a sample performance report.

Your checklist:

- ☐ Review succession planning documents.
- ☐ Review disaster recovery policies.
- ☐ Review advisor and staff resumes.
- ☐ Connect to the advisor's social media accounts (e.g., LinkedIn, Facebook).
- ☐ Review a sample investment policy statement.
- ☐ Review a sample performance report.

Decoding your Advisor's Answers
Core Principle: DUTY

---

1. Can you describe your typical client? (p. 194)

A. An advisor should be able to specifically describe the clients they serve. This matters from a service and staffing standpoint. (Are you too small or too big to be served well by this practice?) Size also matters when it comes to the investment and financial planning expertise the advisor offers for various income and wealth levels, risk profiles, savings and liquidity needs, and investment timelines. You—the potential client—should have a clear sense about what you can and cannot expect from your advisor.

B. A difference in the average assets per client and the typical assets per client can indicate a couple of things: (1) A few large clients skew the numbers, which can potentially mean that the advisor's resources go to serving those large accounts. (2) The advisor does not have a defined client target and is willing to take clients across the income and wealth spectrum, which, as indicated earlier, can mean that you may not get an appropriate level of expertise and service for your needs.

---

2. Can you describe your service profile? (p. 194)

A. It might appear that all clients would want the highest degree of service and technology possible, but that is not always the case. A tech savvy retiree who likes to keep up with the markets on a daily basis might want a high degree of access to their advisor and high-tech access to view their portfolio. Conversely, a busy young couple with small children might only want a quarterly update. There is no right answer to the service question or the technology question, so long as you are getting the service and access to information that meets your needs.

B. Look for a progressive firm that invests in technology and efficiency.

C. There is no single right answer, although some face-to-face meetings are important. More than anything, advisors should be able to describe the level of service clients receive and that service should be frequent enough to make you feel comfortable.

D. Ensure that you won't get lost in the shuffle and that the firm has the staff to handle the work that needs to be done. Compare the advisor-to-client and the support staff-to-client ratios of this firm with the firms of other advisors you interview.

---

3. Will you please provide a list all of the licenses you carry? (p. 195)

A. In many cases advisors carry multiple licenses which allow them to "sell" or advise on different products. This has major implications regarding how they are paid. Cross check the advisor's licenses with their answers below regarding compensation and make sure that they are not getting paid more for certain recommendations than others (e.g., a brokerage license allows someone to charge a commission for trades versus a pure advisor who gets paid a fee for unbiased advice and an insurance license is a dead giveaway that they sell insurance).

---

4. **How do you ensure that your firm remains in compliance with legal and regulatory statutes? (p. 195)**

A. The SEC audits advisors as infrequently as every 10 years. Audits emphasize compliance with laws and regulations but they don't always mean a firm is upholding the highest levels of professionalism. They are the base level of standards, while top advisors far exceed legal standards.

B. Advisor firms should hire auditors to provide mock audits in the typical-long gaps between SEC audits. Every firm should undergo either an SEC or mock audit every three years.

C. The answer you're looking for is "yes." Note that smaller firms often do not use an outside auditor because they lack the resources or initiative to hire one. This is a red flag.

D. You're looking for "yes." An advisor firm should have at least one individual whose job is to ensure that the firm abides by the pertinent rules and regulations.

---

5. **How do you get paid? (p. 196)**

A. This set of questions is all about sniffing out conflicts of interest. Don't put much stock in an advisor's attempts to explain away conflicts of interest.

Remember, there are plenty of advisors whose businesses involve few conflicts or none at all.

B. If an advisor gets paid for selling insurance, he's got a conflict of interest because insurance cannot be sold through a fee arrangement, only a sales commission arrangement. It's usually acceptable for an advisor to evaluate your insurance coverage, as long as you're not being charged a fee for it. If an advisor does sell insurance, the only way for him to eliminate his conflict of interest is to do a "commission offset," reducing your ongoing advisory fee by exactly the amount of the commission he receives on any insurance sale. Similarly, the advisor may recommend mutual funds but its best to manage them as "no-load" under a fee arrangement versus having the advisor receive a commission. When in doubt, the least biased answer is, "No, I get paid a fee for advice not a commission for products."

C. Just like you don't want your doctor to make biased recommendations when prescribing medicine by taking gifts and rewards from pharmaceutical companies, you don't want your advisor to get paid for doing anything other than putting your best interests and financial needs first. Trips, non-cash rewards, or any other real or perceived compensation create biases.

D. Sometimes investment managers will fee share with specific fund companies. Obviously this creates a bias.

E. This is preferable to charging commissions because it eliminates one conflict of interest.

F. A "yes" answer means the advisor has an inherent conflict of interest: Remember, your advisor will be tempted to pay himself a higher fee than is available elsewhere, and he's highly unlikely to fire himself if his performance doesn't stack up.

G. Layers of fees can create conflicts and also make it difficult to understand how your advisor is getting paid. Avoid opaque fee structures where you can.

H. Advisory clients typically pay a range of fees for services like investment transactions, asset custody, mutual fund fees, and so on. Still, you want a totally transparent relationship with your advisor, one in which all of the fees, however minor, are on the table.

Core Principle: SAFEGUARDS

1. **What safeguards does your firm have in place to ensure that my assets are protected from fraud? (p. 199)**

A. Assets should be held with a reputable third-party custodian, rather than being in the advisor's control.

B. Your risk goes up dramatically when your advisor has custody of your money. Serving as a general partner or manager of an LLC is custody. In these cases, it's essential that your advisor use a reputable third-party administrator and a reputable third-party auditor. These outside administrators and auditors play a critical role in providing checks and balances that ensure nothing inappropriate is being done with your assets.

C. You don't want your money invested with the next Bernie Madoff. Madoff got away with his crimes for years because the auditor that provided oversight was not reputable or, ultimately, truly independent. Your advisor should require that any person or firm investing client money should be overseen by a major auditing firm. The firm's job is to ensure that your money is accounted for and is being handled properly.

D. Administrators are responsible for reporting to investors on matters such as contributions, withdrawals, and account balances. The use of a third-party administrator—that is, a company independent from the hedge fund or other asset management firm—means you're far less likely to receive fictional numbers.

E. In discretionary relationships, an advisor is allowed to execute transactions without your approval—you trust him to make the right moves, and can fire him if they don't work out. Most advisory relationships are discretionary. However, a discretionary relationship underscores the importance of using a separate custodian to act as a shield against fraud.

F. The answer should be that the advisor can only wire money with your written permission—usually backed up by a confirming telephone call—to an account under your name only.

G. All your accounts should be held in your name, not your advisor's or anyone else's. If any account is not in your name, you should make sure you understand why.

H. Liability insurance covers cases in which an advisor screws up—putting you in an unsuitable investment, selling a stock they were supposed to buy or forgetting to make a trade, for instance. The right amount of coverage is a subjective matter; $100,000 of coverage per incident might be fine for a firm with an average account size of $50,000, but would be far too low for a firm with an average account size of $100,000. The key here is to compare the coverage levels of the advisors you interview. Low coverage may end up contributing to your decision to rule out a particular advisor. Coverage of $5 million seems appropriate for a small to medium size firm.

I. Nearly every industry provides a privacy policy these days, but it doesn't hurt to read the fine print and understand how and when you information will be used. It's worth asking about how and when your data is passed to affiliated vendors and how the advisory firm monitors their use of personal information.

J. Background checks should be mandatory for employees at most levels of the advisor's organization.

K. A "yes" answer may be a yellow flag, but not necessarily. It may show that the advisor is serious about running a tight ship. If multiple firings have been necessary, there may be more cause for concern.

Core Principle: PROFESSIONALISM

1. What does your firm do to plan for the future? (p. 202)

A. Policies and procedures cannot account for every eventuality but they should demonstrate a thoughtful approach to protecting client's assets and maintaining continuity in times of change or crises.

B. It's important that the company has a succession plan and even insurance to buy out the shares of a major shareholder in the event of an untimely death.

2. Can you please provide a list of your credentials and background? (p. 202)

A. Experience counts, but so do credentials. Don't be afraid to ask hard questions.

B. Advisors need to "stay sharp" on a range of subjects within their industry. The question can help you ascertain that he or she is reading and learning continuously as a way of developing their expertise.

C. You're looking for concrete abilities such as estate planning and/or a sophisticated understanding of areas such as insurance or mortgages. Don't settle for a statement that simply says they offer those services; rather, probe to understand that they truly know what they are talking about.

D. It doesn't matter as much what an advisor's credentials are if less-qualified people will be doing the important work on your account. Know what your team looks like.

E. You want to know that the advisor has invested in being as skilled and capable as possible. You don't just want an advisor selling whatever they can sell. Credentials such as CFA, CFP, CIMA, CPWA, CPA, JD, MBA can help prove that the advisor is serious about his or her professional development.

---

3. Can you explain in plain English your investment process? (p. 203)

A. Investment policy statements describe a client's investment goals and objectives, and lays out how the manager will meet these objectives. A formal, written investment policy statement is a must for a serious advisor. Make sure that it highlights what services you can expect, that it affirmatively states there are no economic conflicts of interest, and that the benchmarks against which each manager is compared is clearly defined.

B. Does the report stand on its own? Meaning, are you able to interpret it without a PhD in finance? A performance report should reflect thoughtful analysis but not be mysterious, intimidating, or overly complex.

C. There is no single right answer to this question. Small firms often use outside research providers, and that arrangement can work perfectly fine. The point is to probe into whether the advisor makes good use of research from a qualified source, rather than choosing investments based on what's hot, or what might benefit him most.

D. The advisor should have a formal evaluation process for hiring and firing investment managers. The absence of such a policy, in writing, means that the advisor may simply sell clients the hot product of the moment without putting much thought into its quality.

E. It's key to ask questions about custody, fees, and any other discretionary activities related to assets managed in house. Generally the thing to think about is whether an advisor will be objective in "firing himself" in the event that investments managed in-house are underperforming. How will he ensure that objectivity?

F. A limited number of investment choices raises a big red flag. You should have access to the best investments available, period. Some advisors will tell you that you do have unlimited choices, but the truth may be that their firm has done you a disservice by narrowing the list of choices down to the best options for them, not you. Be skeptical: When firms narrow their investment options, it's usually based on which investment choices are most lucrative to the firm and to its advisors. As you're comparing firms, you should put plenty of weight on whether a firm offers unlimited investment options. This practice is known in the industry as having "open architecture." Many firms claim to have open architecture but in fact have limited open architecture or a sales pitch that includes words like "open architecture with proprietary products." Conflicts are conflicts, so be aware.

G. To properly vet investment managers, advisors should have an in-house research team of at least five people, or they should use a well-resourced outside investment evaluation service, or both.

After the Interview

Calmly reflect. Never agree to become a client without going home, getting settled, and clearing your head. If your doctor suggested major surgery, you'd likely seek a second opinion and take your time making the decision to move forward. Choosing your investment advisor is equally important.

Go back over your list of questions. Think about whether the candidate's answers were clear and direct. If they made your head spin, that's a red flag. A good advisor can explain complex topics in terms that you can understand and provide backup for every answer.

Cross-check advisor's answers. This is where you need to do your homework. Your "go-to" document is the advisor's Form ADV and/or their marketing materials and sample documents. This is the uniform disclosure document used by investment advisors to register with the SEC. The form consists of two parts. Part 1 uses a check-the-box, fill-in-the-blank format. It's full of key information but can be a grind to decipher— it's designed for use by SEC bureaucrats. You can find it at www.adviserinfo.sec.gov.

Part 2 of the ADV form is to be written in narrative style that describes the firm—including the services it offers, the fees it charges, disciplinary information, conflicts of interest, and the educational and business background of management and key advisory personnel of the advisor. The ADV Part 2 document is available at www.adviserinfo.sec.gov/IAPD/Content/IapdMain/iapd_SiteMap.aspx.

As I've pointed out at length, the disclosure documents that advisors are required to create are often far less than crystal clear. Advisors with conflicts of interest will lard their Form ADV Part 2 with legalese. And that leads to a good rule of thumb: The more difficult it is to decipher a Form ADV Part 2, the greater the likelihood that the advisor has something to hide.

Beware of references and friends. Did the advisor offer references? If so, you should take them with a grain of salt: They're almost guaranteed to be self-serving. If you really want to speak with references, ask for names of *former* clients. Find out why they left and if they're happier where they are now. It's possible that they failed to ask the right questions the first time around. By the way, don't hire a friend as your advisor.

Keep your worlds separate. Sure, you can be friendly with an advisor, but a connection beyond that only makes it more difficult to criticize or leave your advisor if necessary.

There's never an ironclad guarantee that an advisor truly will have your best interests at heart at all times. But doing a thorough screening is a huge step toward improving your odds. And once you commit to an advisor, remember that you can move on if his or her service doesn't match up with their interview responses. You can always fire your advisor—because *you* are the boss.

Key Points

- Most of us don't know the right questions to ask when evaluating an advisor.
- Because of the industry's low barriers to entry, it's possible for one advisor to be great and another to be terrible. There's no minimum standard of competence that we can rely on.
- Any advisor worthy of your consideration should adhere to three solid core principles. These are: (1) Duty—an unwavering loyalty

to clients, (2) Safeguards—a commitment to protect your assets and personal information, and (3) Professionalism—a thoroughly professional approach to doing business.

- The only way to confirm adherence to the three principles is to ask knowledgeable, penetrating questions.
- Use the questions in this chapter to grill prospective advisors. If they're really good, they'll answer directly and persuasively.
- Never engage an advisor without interviewing at least three candidates.
- After you interview an advisor, go home and calmly evaluate his or her responses. Be sure to cross-check as much information as possible using an advisor's Form ADV and other resources.

Chapter 9

Fees and Ice Cream: Baskin-Robbins Got It Right, Why Can't We?

I love ice cream. As a kid, I'd often make a 20-minute bike trek to Baskin-Robbins, where I would deliberate over the famous "31 Flavors" menu of tantalizing combinations. Banana nut fudge, chocolate almond, peppermint stick, eggnog . . . the list seemed to go on and on.

To be honest, I was a pretty predictable customer. I usually ended up going for the mint chocolate chip or just opting for a straight hit of vanilla. But every now and then, I'd throw away the script and choose bubble gum or something more exotic.

Sometimes, you've just got to change it up; you've got to reach beyond the standard fare. Baskin-Robbins figured out a long time ago that variety and flexibility to suit each customer's taste buds at the time of his or her visit was the key to success. It's the reason that particular store, and not the one around the corner, was my go-to ice cream destination. And I wasn't alone.

Imagine, though, if Baskin-Robbins only offered chocolate and vanilla, and maybe an occasional strawberry "special." That wouldn't be worth biking out of your way for, and it doesn't sound like the recipe for a successful business, does it?

Yet this is exactly what the financial advisor industry has done. For years, advisors have offered two or three flavors of fee arrangements, ignoring the fact that investors' situations and needs are much more diverse.

There's chocolate and vanilla for a reason . . . choice matters.

When we're stuck with a fee "flavor" that doesn't match our needs, we usually end up paying too much, and we have a harder time meeting our goals. In almost every category of things we can buy, the U.S. consumer expects choice—the more the better. But when it comes to financial advice, we've become accustomed to a tiny and strangely truncated menu. The good news is that consumers don't have to settle for it.

Chocolate and Vanilla

Investment advisors typically charge clients in one of three ways: (1) fees as a percentage of assets under management (AUM); (2) commissions or other compensation from product manufacturers; or, (3) flat fees—either an hourly charge or an annual retainer. Let's quickly review how these approaches work.

AUM-Based Fees

In this model, the advisor charges you a fee based on a percentage of your assets under his or her management. The advisor has an incentive to increase your account value and minimize losses, since he or she earns more as your assets grow. Typical asset-management fees range from more than 2 percent per year to 0.5 percent per year. Generally speaking, the more assets you have, the lower the fee as a percentage of your billable assets. Something to watch out for is a "land grab" if you use multiple advisors who are paid in this fashion. Each will have perverse incentive to undermine the strategy of the other advisor in the hopes of advising on your entire pool of assets. This issue creates its own unique conflict of interest.

Commissions

Brokers are most often paid commissions from the investment or insurance company whose products they sell. Sales commissions come in any number of forms; a common commission is the up-front sales load on a mutual fund.

Hourly and Retainer Fees

Certain advisors charge an hourly rate for providing advice or creating a full financial plan, with the expectation that implementing the guidance is up to the client. Some advisors charge certain clients a quarterly or annual retainer fee to provide ongoing advice. In both cases, clients like the compensation models because they're seen as conflict-free.

Baskin-Robbins ⅔ 3 Flavors?

Rocky road, pecan, mint chocolate chip—we all have our own tastes in ice cream. Likewise, as investors, we all have different, specific needs. Today I cater to some of the wealthiest Americans—folks used to virtually unlimited choice in almost every facet of their life. Yet when it comes to investment advice, their choice is limited to chocolate or vanilla; they can pay me a percentage of their assets or a flat rate. That's how they have been conditioned by the industry, and I have certainly played my part in creating this outcome.

The truth is that no two clients require the same service or bring the same complexity to a relationship. Consider two very typical examples, both involving wealthy families.

1. Client A has $50 million of assets divided among five family members. Each family member is married, each has his or her individual goals, and each has unique estate planning needs. Adding to the complexity of this relationship, a few of the family members are "old school"—that is, they prefer paper reports and face-to-face meetings on a quarterly basis. The final wrinkle is that the family matriarch likes to hang out with her wealthy friends and swap stories about the family's hedge fund and private equity successes (leaving out the failures, of course). In other words, illiquid investments are a staple of the family's portfolio.

2. Client B, meanwhile, has a $100 million portfolio. But this relationship is low-maintenance. The client, a successful tech entrepreneur, is single and in his late twenties. Not surprisingly, he is

tech-centric—in fact, he wants to see his performance reports on his iPad, and he loves having meetings over the Internet.

In the vanilla AUM model, each of these clients pays according to the amount of assets their advisor oversees. That means our 20-something entrepreneur is effectively penalized. Client A's advisors have to travel to meet with the old-school family members. They have to produce paper reports. Meetings with each individual family member are required. The family requires estate planning, and its portfolio is full of more complex types of alternative investments.

It's evident that the relatively low-maintenance client should pay less than the family with fewer assets and much more complexity, but that's not the case.

If the AUM model is the vanilla approach, what about serving these clients chocolate—a flat rate—instead? In that case, other challenges present themselves. As it turns out, Client B is likely to enjoy another significant liquidity event in the coming years when he sells thousands of shares of stock in the company he founded. How should his advisor account for the additional assets under the fixed-fee model?

The effort required to service the client won't increase as a result of his windfall, but the amount of money under advisement would rise substantially. And that increase in assets will bring increased risk. Losing 10 percent on a $100 million portfolio costs twice as much as losing 10 percent on a $50 million portfolio, after all (particularly if there's an error in the account; and errors do happen). And what if Client B gets married and needs estate planning? Or what if he makes any number of decisions in the years ahead that add complexity to his account?

Now let's look at Client A. At first glance, finding a flat fee that corresponds to the complexity of the account seems like a straightforward matter. But there's a competitive issue—the flat fee may look outsized when compared with the off-the-rack rate charged by rival advisors. The competing advisor might very well be bluffing when he claims to offer similar services for that lower price. But remember, most advisory clients *don't know what they don't know*.

In fact, that advisor may be less focused on providing the best possible advice than he is on persuading clients to move all of their assets to his firm.

But the typical investor probably wouldn't be savvy enough to see through the advisor's motives. Too often even the wealthiest consumers fall for salesmanship, passing over the right advisor for a rival who offers a smoother pitch and perhaps what seems to be a better deal. Client A's advisor knows this very well, and, as a result, he may think twice before proposing a flat fee.

We haven't even touched on the "strawberry" alternative yet. My firm doesn't serve that flavor. But brokers do, under the hopelessly conflicted model in which they earn commissions for selling investments or insurance.

The current menu of choices is a Neapolitan mess! Why can't you just get your favorite flavor? Why isn't there a fee arrangement that neatly fits your needs?

Key Pricing Ingredients (Building a Custom Sundae)

There are a few key factors that should go into pricing every relationship. Each factor should reflect the work and the risk involved in that relationship. And each should distance the advisor from conflicts of interest to the fullest possible extent. The key factors are:

- *Value*—The core ingredient in a relationship. An advisor's value to a client rests on factors such as crafting the right financial plan, innovating and proactively addressing estate planning and tax considerations when appropriate, providing discipline in volatile markets, or conveying information on investment strategies with which a client is unfamiliar.

- *Complexity*—Are the accounts invested completely in exchange-traded funds or index mutual funds? Or are there active managers, such as active mutual funds or separate account managers? Are hedge funds among the recommended investments? Each of these nuances requires the advisory firm to have more and more expensive resources to service the client relationships, and this cost should be passed on to the client.

- *Reporting (custodians)*—Using a single custodian and simplified, online reporting keeps costs down. Add in alternative assets, multiple custodians, multiple owners (e.g., trusts, IRAs, and other types of accounts), and the cost of reporting can skyrocket. The account's pricing should reflect this complexity.

- *Service level*—The online advisors described earlier in this book can service tens of thousands of clients through automated systems. The clients I work with often want to see me and speak with me at their leisure and often for considerable amounts of time. Increased levels of service require larger, more qualified staff. This additional cost should be factored into pricing.

These pricing components won't remain static over the years within a client/advisor relationship. As they change, pricing should move in tandem, reflecting a client's changing needs and the advisor's changing responsibilities and risks. Investors should pay no more than the cost of the services and research that they require, and no less than the cost of the services and research that they use.

Baskin-Robbins really can teach us something about choice. And that brings us to Chapter 10, which considers the future of the industry, and you.

Chapter 10

Change the Game

Twenty years ago, if you wanted to buy a book or a pair of shoes, you went to a store, made your purchase, and drove home. From time to time, you might order something from a catalogue—a power tool perhaps, or a pair of pajamas. Back then, most of us simply could not conceive of another way to shop.

But while you and I were schlepping to Sears to buy a new vacuum cleaner or a six-pack of socks, a former hedge fund executive named Jeff Bezos was working out of his garage, starting the company that would become Amazon.com.

Spoiler Alert:

Amazon today is a $100-billion empire that has revolutionized the way we buy books, tools, toys, and just about everything else. Bezos has been hailed by *Fortune* magazine as the "ultimate disruptor." And Sears and all the other retailers who have been disrupted have been scrambling to catch up.

A couple of decades ago, electric cars existed only in science fiction. Today, tens of thousands of hybrid gas/electric cars are on the road, and pure electric cars are a reality. Elon Musk, probably the best-known champion of electric cars and the founder of Tesla, is also spearheading an effort to develop civilian space travel capabilities. Richard Branson, known for his Virgin brands fame, is doing the same.

And we've already talked about how discount online-brokerage revolutionized the financial industry in the 1970s and how software-based investing is pushing the envelope even further today. Look at what Steve Jobs did in only a few years with the iPad and iPhone. The world is changing at an ever-accelerating pace.

Take a step back and you'll see that the list of services and goods that have moved from fantasy to reality over the past decade is impressive. And that's why I believe that, even though the advisory world of today seems to be locked into the same old flavors when it comes to pricing, new items will soon be on the menu. And that change will likely be here before most of the industry is able to react.

The change that is coming to financial services pricing isn't as sexy as space travel and it won't give you an ice cream sugar high or even satisfy your cravings. But as a practical matter, it will make a huge difference in your family's financial wellbeing.

New ways of doing things will emerge because visionaries within the industry have shown that they are possible, and because consumers at every level along the wealth spectrum ultimately will vote with their dollars for progress, transparency, and fair pricing.

I predict that in less than a decade, the following three changes will be firmly in place:

1. Separation of value services from commodity services.

Once upon a time, airline travel was a luxury reserved for the well-to-do. Today, with numerous airlines competing for your business, air travel is the standard way to traverse long distances, and it's available to virtually everyone. In other words, air travel has become a commodity, and pricing (and the ability to shop online for flights based on price) reflects this change.

The world of financial advice has its commodities, too. They include guidance about which investments to buy and how to mix different types of asset classes within your portfolio. These aspects of financial advice (i.e., asset allocation and fund/manager/stock selection) are now standard across the industry, and should be assigned relatively low cost to reflect the fact that they are commodity services. I submit that if you line up the top 50, 100, or even 500 firms and gave them the same client to plan for, 20 years from now the investment portfolio results would be amazingly similar.

The data suggests that there are few consistent, outstanding stock pickers and investment fund managers—so few that they are as uncommon as airplane crashes. So, sticking with my analogy, Warren Buffett is one of those outstanding asset managers; and everyone knows Warren Buffett's name because he is one of a kind. He is (when it comes to newsworthiness) the equivalent of a space shuttle disaster—it almost never happens. However, the manager of a middle-of-the-pack mutual fund is the equivalent of an on-time JetBlue departure.

On the other hand, the best advisors—the top decile—deliver an enormous amount of value when they provide unconflicted and customized guidance and information about complex financial planning, taxes, and estate planning situations. They provide value when they keep you from making imprudent decisions. This kind of advice is a world away from being a commodity.

A great advisor and a run-of-the-mill advisor will often provide pretty much the same commodity when it comes to asset allocation and investment recommendations. But a truly *excellent* advisor can add quantum value to your family's net worth through the non-commodity of quality advice.

Today, pricing does not reflect the commodity-services/value-services divide. An advisor might provide asset allocation and investment recommendations to one client and complex advice to another, and charge them the same fee. But before long, the consumer who buys a commodity service will pay less, and the consumer who receives a value service will pay a value-oriented fee.

As pricing shifts to reflect the specific level of complexity and risk within an advisor-client relationship, the rigid vanilla/chocolate/strawberry model will start to melt away. And pricing will become clear and straightforward—more like the pricing in a grocery store. Both commodity services and value services will have clear price tags. They won't be mixed together and assigned an arbitrary price.

2. A focus on unconflicted advice from capable fiduciaries.

Consumers will increasingly appreciate and demand the services of advisors who are capable, whose advice is unbiased, and who are fiduciaries. And they will ultimately be able to tell the difference. As I suggested earlier, people who sell products should be clearly identified and people who provide only advice clearly delineated, too. (*You may recall that I suggested people with conflicts should be called brokers and true fiduciaries should be called advisors.*)

Today, the brokerage model is still dominant in the financial advice industry. But the winds of change are already starting to blow. In recent years, hundreds if not thousands of advisors have left the conflicted world of brokerage firms to become independent RIAs in order to better serve clients.

And clients have been yanking their money from marquee-name brokerage firms like UBS, Merrill Lynch, Wells Fargo, and Morgan Stanley Smith Barney, and moving it to RIAs with much lower profiles. As I explained previously, while RIA firms don't have a fraction of the visibility that the dominant brokerages do, this is likely to change. Today, the industry is made up of over 15,000 independent firms, and that makes for a serious marketing challenge. Too few people know the difference between brokers and fiduciaries such as RIAs. And even fewer can tell the capable, true fiduciaries from those posing as such. However, information technology can rapidly change this. And many fiduciary advisors are trying to get the word out on what it means to do the right thing.

But the main reason I'm confident that fiduciaries are the future is because I have faith in the American consumer. Conflicted, self-serving non-fiduciaries will only be able to beguile consumers for so long. Eventually investors large and small will see through the slick marketing campaigns and glossy brochures of golden retrievers and sailboats and decide that they deserve solid, objective advice from able practitioners who are sworn to put clients' interests first.

3. Partner firms that empower consumers will emerge.

As the vanilla/chocolate/strawberry status quo is replaced by a marketplace full of options and flexibility, a brand-new category of fiduciaries will spring up to help consumers make the best choices.

These partner firms will help you to figure out which model you need, which advisor or resource to go to, and how much you should be paying. The best partner firms will not only recommend investment partners but will audit advisors to ensure that they are highly qualified, highly professional, and committed to your interests first and foremost.

This new breed of firm will represent a major evolutionary step in the financial services industry. Until the early 1990s, professional investment advice was almost exclusively provided through brokers. As consultants and "managers of managers" became popular, the number of independent advisors skyrocketed. Those independent advisors stood between the brokerage firms and custodians that housed and handled investment portfolios and transactions, as well as the asset managers who ran mutual funds, separately managed accounts, and other products.

The emerging firm of the future will oversee the tens of thousands of RIAs, brokers, and other advisors who all claim to be the best partner for you, segregating these firms by the qualities that best meet your needs. The new, pure fiduciary advisors will provide unconflicted, expert financial planning, and tax and estate advice, and help steer you through the cluttered and confusing landscape to find exactly the advisor you need to execute the more commoditized portion of the plan—asset allocation and manager selection.

Why Wait?

The nice thing about change in the financial services industry is that, just like an electric car, consumers can drive it, starting now. Consumers can urge Elon Musk or Richard Branson to hurry up and develop civilian spacecraft, but that probably won't speed up the process. However, if consumers throw their weight around with advisors—demanding to be treated fairly with respect to conflicts and pricing—advisors will acquiesce.

Remember Client B from Chapter 9, the one with the $100 million portfolio? Imagine him sitting down with his advisor and explaining that, while he appreciates that the advisor charges 0.75 percent annually against his assets under management, that's not the way he wants to pay for the service. Do you think that advisor would show his $100-million, low-maintenance client the door? Or would he suggest a conversation about a more customized approach?

I know for a fact that a number of firms are researching ways to charge clients based on complexity and risk rather than the rigid old formulas. The more consumers demand this change, the faster the industry will adopt it.

And this doesn't just go for ultra-wealthy people like Client B. Even investors whom many advisors see as too small can shape the future of the industry through the choices they make. Why not ditch your advisor and use an ultra-low-cost software-based investing service such as Wealthfront or Betterment (to repeat my disclosure from earlier in the book, I'm an investor in the latter)?

Those sites handle asset allocation and investment selection—commodity services, if you'll recall—for low, commodity-like prices. If your advisor isn't giving you value-added guidance on top of his or her commodity advice, consider making the jump and saving money. If your advisor is really adding value, let's say by keeping you from making financial decisions that you know are counterproductive, then that's another story. But as we've discussed, too many advisors are *yes-men*, content to collect fees and acquiesce to whatever their clients want. They are simply overpriced gatekeepers to the over-hyped mysterious world of manager selection and asset allocation.

A funny thing happens when consumers refuse to overpay. They can change the very way that industries do business. Consumer power is behind the success of Walmart and other big-box stores that, like Amazon, have disrupted the old, more-expensive, department store model. It's behind the success of discount brokerages like Charles Schwab and E*Trade. And I'm convinced that consumers will help to speed the change that's coming to the financial advice industry.

Afterword

Advisors
in Perspective

Many people believe that investing means
putting their money behind specific
companies, or more generally putting it
to work "in the market." I believe that investors
should always keep a broader view in mind: What we
really invest in is *capitalism* itself.

Capitalism is an engine of prosperity that's bigger than any one company or even one country. The beautiful thing is that we all have access to this wealth-creating force, as entrepreneurs, workers, or investors. When we invest money, we're reflecting our belief in capitalism. We're expressing confidence that it can—and will—lift us into greater prosperity over time.

As investors, we often take it as a given that the way to tap into the potential of capitalism is through our financial advisor. But we have to remember that any investing success we enjoy ultimately comes from capitalism itself and not from an advisor. The advisor's job is to be a useful guide, helping us to tap into the creative power of capitalism in an intelligent and disciplined way. If an advisor is not acting as a guide, he or she has not earned the right to your business.

Advisors should understand that they don't make money for clients. The markets do that. Capitalism does that. And no advisor is the sole gatekeeper to the markets. No advisor should ever treat their responsibilities casually, and no advisor should ever enrich themselves at the expense of their customers.

If I control the only bridge over a raging river, I can charge a fee every time you want to cross that river. I don't have to do anything but take your money. Too often, advisors act like gatekeepers of a bridge to the markets. They collect a fee and often do little or nothing to help their customers. Sometimes they even collect more in fees than they're entitled to because their clients don't know of another route to get to their destination.

The good news is that there are thousands of bridges into the markets. And there is an advisor standing at each bridge or manning some vessel to speed you across. You, the consumer, have the luxury of choosing the advisor you'll work with. You have the power to ignore any advisor who isn't superbly qualified to help you accomplish your goals and 100 percent committed to serving your best interests. Thanks to discount online brokerages and other technology, you even have the power to be your own advisor if you so choose.

Many advisors have yet to perceive the extent to which technology and the power of consumer choice have made them expendable. They seem to believe that they're doing you a favor by letting you be their client. They seem not to understand that they're just one of many ways for you to access the markets, to access the power of capitalism. And they will likely be in for a rude awakening as technology continues to democratize access to investment advice.

On the other hand, there are many advisors who understand exactly what's going on. They know that in exchange for your fees, they've got to deliver the *goods*. They have to develop and sustain real expertise that can serve you—not just in investing, but in other dimensions of your financial life, such as taxes and financial or estate planning. They have to be committed to work in your best interests at all times, and not to *nickel and dime* you through hidden fees. They have to make clear to you, the consumer, exactly what they're providing and exactly what you'll pay for it, and they must never use legalese to hide conflicts of interest.

Wised-up, empowered consumers are helping to tip the scales toward a future where advisors truly deserve our trust. And you can be a part of it, starting right now.

About the Author

Steve Lockshin founded Convergent Wealth Advisors in 1994 to deliver a differentiated offering to ultra-affluent individuals. Steve served as CEO of the firm for 18 years, during which time Convergent became one of the nation's leading wealth management firms, providing investors with objective advice, flexible investment solutions, and complete transparency.

Recognized as a thought leader in the wealth management industry, Steve helped pioneer the open architecture approach to investing. He was also an early adopter of asset allocation strategies for the ultra-high-net-worth client, employing a mathematical process to determine appropriate client portfolios based on cash flow needs. With Steve's oversight, Convergent became an innovator in the use and analysis of risk and reward parameters for alternative portfolios, equity risk management for concentrated portfolio holdings, and other strategies now employed industry-wide.

Steve has received many industry accolades, including being ranked by *Barron's* as the #1 advisor in California for the past two years. Steve ranked #2 on *Barron's* Top 100 Independent Financial Advisors list in 2012 and #1 in 2011, his third straight year as one of the top five independent advisors in the nation. In 2010, *Washingtonian Magazine* named Steve as one of the Top Financial Advisors in the Washington, DC area.

In 1995, as part of the development of Convergent Wealth Advisors, Steve founded CMS Reporting. CMS Reporting is now known as Fortigent, LLC, a leading provider of outsourced wealth management solutions with over $50 billion in assets on its platform.

Steve earned a Bachelor of Science degree from the University of Maryland. He also holds the Investment Management Consultants Association's Certified Investment Management Analyst (CIMA®) designation and the Investment Strategist Certificate (ISC), as well as the Financial Industry Regulatory Authority (FINRA) Series 7, 63, and 65 licenses. He is a long-time member of the Young Presidents Organization (YPO). Steve is also an accomplished pilot, graduating from his private pilot certificate to piloting corporate jets in less than three years.

Index